Lessons Learned........A Teacher's Memoir

By: Cheryl Gordon Cofer

Dedication

I dedicate this book to my mother, Mrs. Shirley B. Grier. Thanks for encouraging me to finalize my thoughts and teaching memories into a book. You have always been my biggest cheerleader! Thanks for your unwavering love and support.

Foreward

God has a way of granting us such amazing things. I have been privileged to be granted a sibling that is truly an angel because of the lives that she has touched during her years on this earth. At a very young age, Cheryl Gordon Cofer demonstrated signs of being a top notch leader because of her understanding, calm, and enduring demeanor. The fond memories that she was able to capture during her many years of educating students are phenomenal. This book will definitely help all readers to deal with unexpected and difficult situations. It will give a clear understanding of what it takes to truly educate individuals. Teachers, use it wisely. It will remind you of just how great the profession is. Teaching is what you make it!

Pamela Nanette Gordon

Acknowledgements

This book has been a long time in the making. I would like to take this opportunity to thank all of the people who are responsible for making this book possible.

I wish to thank my Lord and Savior for giving me the gift of teaching and the mindset to recall so many precious memories. I thank my family for all of their continuous love and support. A special thanks to all of my friends, co-workers, and students for giving me most of the material included in this book.

Finally, a special shout out to my cousin Pam, niece Keidrian, daughter in law Kelora and Soror, Dr. Louise Rice for their special attention in helping me to finalize this book.

Introduction

A few months ago, I turned forty and I realized a lot about me had changed: my weight, my family, and especially my memory. It seems strange how there are some things that just stick with you for years while others can't be recalled an hour later. One thing that has not changed is my love for teaching. When I start reminiscing about teaching, I realize that there are just some things I will never forget and that over the years, I learned as much as I taught. With this in mind, I'd like to share the many memories that I recall. I am amazed at what I remember. Maybe you will be also.

Table of Contents

Despise not small beginnings......

Zechariah 4:10

1

A Lesson In Hope

It was an ordinary Monday morning in October 1982. Unfortunately for me, my ordinary was waking up to go to work at my mall job, even though I had just graduated with a college degree in Early Childhood Education. I thought my ordinary would consist of prepping my classroom, greeting precious young children in the morning, and helping their bright young minds understand the wonderful world that was all around them. I had my lesson plans all laid out in my head. I knew how I would introduce our newest section on colors. I could see their backpacks hanging up in the corner of the classroom and their little coats hanging on the racks. But wait, reality check, that wasn't my ordinary. Considering all of those things only aggravated me. They were a reminder that another week had gone by without me being hired.

The reality was I had been looking for a teaching position all summer, but I just couldn't land one. Oh, there were several openings in the county, and just when I thought I was close to getting one, I was informed that they had met their quota for black teachers, now that really stung!

The morning started out as usual. I was in the shower when I received a phone call from a Director at the Board of Education. She told me there was a position available at Kipling Elementary School. My aunt taught there and I was very familiar with the school. So, with a mixture of excitement and anxiousness, I told the Director I was interested in the position. It all happened so fast I hardly had time to digest what I had just heard. I was excited and anxious all at the same time. I thought to myself, "Could I possibly be this blessed? Is this the reason that I wasn't hired earlier?" After all of the interviews, worry, and doubt, it finally came through. The Lord had *this* position waiting for me the whole time. And it was perfect.

I had to remind myself to actually listen to what the lady was saying to me. She told me that I needed to go to Kipling today for an interview, and you'd better believe I went. I woke up that morning thinking I was going to my mall job, but instead I may actually have been finally getting my dream job. So, I got dressed and headed straight to Kipling Elementary School, not my mall job. My ordinary was finally fixed.

I interviewed with the principal, Mr. Craften, and the interview went exceptionally well. Here was a man that heralded the joys of teaching and cherished children. He was honest and forthright and an excellent leader. His aura immediately drew me in and I knew I wanted to work there; not because I wanted my first teaching job, but because his charisma met me at the door and I believed that with him at the helm, we could positively impact the lives of students. I was inspired and assured Mr. Craften that I was the one for the job. He liked me and told me I would be hearing from him very soon.

He called the next morning and said he wanted to hire me, but he had been instructed to hire a white woman. The woman who left the previous position was black but the Board told the principal that the next teacher needed to be a white one. No, not the quota thing again! All of my hopes and dreams were perched on the edge just waiting to jump off. I was deflated. I mean, why did I even go to college? I was trapped in the roar of my thoughts and my mind nearly exploded all over again, but hope calmed me down. And his next words to me were, "Don't give up yet. If there is a way to hire you, I will. Just give me a few days."

I immediately started praying. All I could think about was getting my first teaching job in a secure environment. My aunt and all of her friends worked there - people who had known me as a child and had seen me grow up. Everyone I met at this school seemed to be loving and it appeared to be the ideal place to start a career. "Lord", I prayed, "please let me get this job!"

Tuesday went by and, of course, I couldn't wait to call Mr. Craften on Wednesday. He assured me that he hadn't hired anyone and that he would do everything in his power to "hold out" until the Board of Education allowed him to hire me. Being a principal of more than 24 years, I felt he had quite a bit of power, so I tried to feel relaxed, praying continuously.

Wednesday and Thursday came and went. My mother, who was also a teacher, immediately made telephone contacts with Board members and eventually the Superintendent. I'm not sure what happened but between my prayers, Mom's calls, and the principal's bargaining, I was hired. At the close of the day on Friday, Mr.

Craften called me with excitement in his voice and asked me if I was ready to work. I screamed; was I ever ready!!! That weekend did not go by fast enough. All I could think about was all the things I would do once I got into my very own classroom!

I was quite nervous about greeting the kids. Sure they were six-year-olds and I was 21, but I was actually scared - not a bad scared but a good scared! This scared feeling of excitement is something I would experience prior to the first day of school for the next thirty plus years.

The first day went wonderfully. There were twenty-nine students, ten who were repeating first grade and nine who should have still been in kindergarten. My work was certainly cut out for me. I had a teaching assistant that had probably been there since the school was built. She loved doing art and making beautiful bulletin boards and spent most of her time working on these items, sitting at her desk! She was nice, but did not involve herself much with academics or discipline. My classroom always looked great due to her creativity, however, there is more to teaching besides a pretty classroom…much more. I, on the other hand, was HARD; a lack of discipline was not tolerated. I absolutely, positively ate, slept, and drank teaching. I arrived early and left late every day. At night, I dreamed of ways to make what I had done the previous day better.

I can still remember a lot of the students that made up that first class. There was one girl who was always absent due to some type of illness; two girls had the same name, "Melody". One had beautiful hazel brown eyes; the other was left-handed and sucked her thumb. Also, there was a tall girl who was really quiet. I had two boys that were best friends – Reid and Dean. Dean's parents had me in the office more than once for one reason or another. He wore a hearing aid and always used this to say he didn't hear me, but this was his way of ignoring me. There was also my wild-child, Audrian, who told me right away that teachers can't spank kids without parents' permission. Little did she know, her mother had already signed and given me written permission to do what was necessary, you should have seen the look on her face when she found out. Then there was my little boy who could do no wrong, Willie. Whatever I asked, he did, never giving me any trouble. There was Bailey who was also a sweetheart. And how could I forget "little man" who appeared to be unkept. His clothes were usually worn and he had a hard time with his work, but he was sweet, obedient, and never bothered anyone. Tristen was in this class too. He was a repeater —but he was darling. He had given his previous teachers a fit, but not me. He was my helper and assisted me for a couple of years. He was really good to have around. He could run errands and get messages relayed correctly. And boy could he clean! He kept our classroom neat and tidy, another thing in which I took pride. (We never let the classroom get too out-of-hand).

Two of my repeaters, Tristen and Dwight, obviously retained because of behavior, taught me one of my first lessons I would learn; - **Do not allow a child to fail due to his/her behavior.** Dwight – boy, was he slick. He spent most of his day clowning and not getting his work done. He broke me in. I can't say there's ever been another student quite like him. I have run into many of these students, but not him. I often wonder whatever became of him. My sweet, quiet girls – Netra and my name sake, Sharon; Anthony, Lacey, LaShondra, and Thomas were also there.

The student that sticks out most was my BD student. (BD was an acronym for Behavior Disorder in the 80's). He was eight years old and still in first grade. I was warned about him by other teachers as soon as I took the job. He kept me on my toes. He was in my dreams. He was almost as tall as I was and smart. He had actually been kept back for not getting his work done.

Overall, the class was well behaved and taught me early that students have to be dealt with individually because everyone's different. Fortunately, I could leave that class, go down the hall to the office, come back and they would still be sitting there working quietly. This was really great considering there were twenty-nine first graders in one room with a disciplinarian teacher and a teacher assistant who was not concerned about discipline. She did make some things easier for me, however, and I was very appreciative of what she did do.

My principal and I both considered my first year to be a success!!! I can't end the first year without speaking about my principal and I do mean mine! I had been on dozens of interviews, but Mr. Craften believed in me from day one and gave me a chance. I will always be grateful to him for that. He did not "play". He knew how to run a school. He was visible, demanded respect, and got it. There was never a discipline problem that wasn't handled immediately. He evidently hired teachers that he believed in and he backed them. He was always in classrooms observing and used the observations to make his school better. If teachers didn't want to teach – they either had to improve or hit the road! Under Mr. Craften's leadership, there was never any running in the halls by students and lunch was so peaceful. I miss those days. Regardless of the situation, Mr. Craften backed me and under no circumstances would he ever allow parents to disrespect me. That meant so much.

Oh how I admire the way he ran that school. I learned a lot just by watching the way he handled different situations. He was a great supervisor under whom to start a teaching career. Unfortunately, he retired after my first year, but I had the opportunity to see him several times afterwards. In the numerous times that he returned to the school for special programs, he never failed to ask about the "the young teacher that it took a week to hire."

At the end of my first year, I was hit with some bad luck. Richmond County had a surplus of teachers, especially Black ones. The last twenty-seven teachers hired in the county could not return. Having been hired in late October, you can guess who had to go. Although I would really miss everyone at Kipling Elementary, I was down but not out. Prayer got me through it.

A few weeks before school was scheduled to begin, I was offered a first grade position at a school about five minutes from the previous one, and so I thought, "At least I have a job." since I had just gotten married. Fortunately, God was not finished with me yet:

within a few days of school opening, a first grade teacher who had been at Kipling Elementary for years, suddenly quit. Talk about a blessing! I immediately called the new principal and asked for an interview. Although I was granted an interview, he quickly let me know that my previous work there meant very little and that he would call me in a few days if, in fact, I was chosen. Did he burst my bubble quickly, but God stepped right in and in a few days I got that call. I was back!!!

2

A Lesson In Friendship

The second year was quite different. I don't even know where to begin. Our new principal changed all of the school rules. Whatever the previous principal had done, he wanted it done just the opposite. Students no longer walked on that "magical" center line that worked so well, the lunch room was no longer quiet, and the list goes on. He was constantly in my face about something; your bulletin board went up late, you turned in a form late. He totally ignored the fact that I was giving it all I had basically by myself.

He hired some other new first grade teachers and moved me to another hall away from them. He also placed the most difficult students in my classroom. I didn't realize this until later because I was just glad to be back. I had about ten students who should have been retained in kindergarten but weren't. Three of these students would eventually be accepted into the special education program. They talked and giggled at everything all day. I remember a sweet little fellow who **could read, but couldn't hear sounds** – that blew me away. This was another one of those **lessons** for me. **It was the first experience where I worked with a child that relied totally on memory to recall words.** He was a pretty good reader but his comprehension skills suffered. I definitely had to come up with different and creative ways to work with him. I also remember Teddy, a good student with a quick temper. He would fight if you looked at him too long. I had a girl who just agreed with everything you said, never actually understanding what was going on. Unfortunately, I never met a lot of their parents. Many of them just put their child on the bus the first day of school and that was it. That was another wake-up call for me. Oh, did I mention I became pregnant two months after I got married, I was sick as a dog. I ended up being hospitalized for dehydration. To top it off, the school was being painted and the smell of paint kept me nauseated. What a year!!! Most of it was a blur.

I also had the pleasure of getting another one of those Stewart brothers – Colby, who was Tristen' brother and even sweeter than Tristen. I had watched him give his kindergarten teacher a fit. I couldn't wait to make him obey. (I forgot to mention Tristen had a little temper.) Colby was just the opposite and was happy-go-lucky. He had misbehaved only because he had been allowed to do so. I had no problems with him at all unless he thought I was ignoring him. This didn't happen often. Colby made me realize (an important **lesson)** that most small children will do whatever you allow them or expect them to do. I would see the Stewart boy's mother every now and then; it is always a wonderful reunion. She always remembered me and made me feel appreciated.

That year could not end fast enough. By the end of summer, that principal was gone, I had a beautiful baby girl, and I was back and looking forward to a new year.

Year three brought about more changes. I got a new teacher assistant and was moved to another classroom. This was directly in front of the office. A few months into the school year, I got my third principal. This principal meant business and we hit it off immediately. He knew how to talk to people and get work out of them. My teacher assistant, Ms. Oscar, was an English major with one grown son. We would spend our free time talking about our children, mostly how to get my child to eat. Finally, I knew what it was like to have someone else in the class that "had my back", review what I   taught, and remind misbehaving students of the rules. It was a refreshing change!!! We became close friends and worked as a team. The students knew it and there was no getting over on us. We taught our butts off.

Students I remember from year three covered the gamut. One student rode a cab to school. There was a group of students that were bussed in from the inner-city who could "go to work". The names Randy, Miranda, LaDawn, Abigail, and Maurice come to mind. Active but smart, they challenged me daily. If I could keep their little minds busy, they wouldn't be any trouble. LaDawn still calls me to this day. Abigail was a straight genius. Miranda couldn't be still but was so cute. There was a male thumb sucker in this group and a little-bitty girl who walked to school. She was the first to express her future career as being a "momma". Another wake-up call. **Lesson here: All moms do not work outside of the home. Also, those mommies that are at home DO WORK!**

Bailey was in this class. He was so excited to be able to give me red earrings. This was rare, because most of my students couldn't afford to buy gifts for their teachers. There was Patrick whom I had watched in kindergarten giving his teachers a fit, along with Netra, Janice, Akeem, and others.

Anita was my biggest challenge for that year. She was a twin and not the "good one". She was almost as tall as me, mean as a snake and smart. Though she was one of my top achievers, she never wanted to work. She was continuously finding ways to get out of work. We could not go from my desk to the door without getting into an altercation. I refused to allow her behavior to keep her back or get the best of me. For every problem she conjured up for me, I would go home and think of a solution. I would constantly tell her that she would get tired before I would. What she didn't know is that every time I heard her read or actually got her to complete any task, she drove me to work harder. By the end of the year, she was willfully completing her classwork and staying out of trouble. I had won her over.

Also, one of my favorite cousin, MeMe was hired down the hall from me this year. Because we needed a teacher assistant in kindergarten, MeMe, was hired after I recommended her to my principal. He liked her, hired her, and never regretted it. Again, I experienced another successful year because of children that worked hard and responded well to my teaching and discipline style. I also had a teacher assistant, parents and a principal that trusted and supported me. Life was good! To top things off, The Cosby Show began airing sometime during that year. After all it took for me to get my teaching position, it was a nice change to finally see a television show that did not diminish the roles of African-Americans.

The next year Ms. Oscar and I were still together in yet another classroom. I had finally gotten back in the vicinity of the other first grade classrooms. This was a nice and much more convenient. I was also right next to the library and one door away from the teachers' rest room! Oh how I appreciated this, because this was a big deal for teachers. It looked like the tag team was at it again, but unfortunately for me and fortunate for Ms. Oscar, she was offered a teaching position and she took it.

This school year would change my life forever. With another new principal I was introduced to my best friend for life, Diana Barnes. The year began with no teacher assistant and my second and final pregnancy. One day early in the school year, I was called to the office to meet the new teacher assistant for my class. There I met a woman about my height who looked to be about my age and the no-nonsense type. I took one look at her and thought, "She doesn't look friendly or like she wants to work". Could I EVER have been more wrong!! After leaving the office we hit it off within minutes. Never had I had a teacher assistant who was so in tuned with my system. I went over my techniques with her once and from then on it was as though she read my mind. I could be thinking of what needed to be done next and she would already be in the process of preparing for it. This class was trying, also. Not only was she a good assistant, she was a good teacher-for me as well as the students. I even became more affectionate because she taught me so much about life, love, and Godly things I thought I already knew. **Another lesson learned here. I finally learned how to be flexible and lighten up with my students and still have success in the classroom.** Before Diana, there was no bending. If I made a threat due to bad behavior, it was ALWAYS carried out. My no-bend policy eventually disappeared. We had a large class that year, but we worked hard and got positive results.

This was the first year, I think, that I became seriously attached to my students. Carl was my baby. He stole my heart. Also, there were Riley, Cordel, Mark, Kendra, Sherri, Carol, Roco, Shantay, Charlie, Detrick, and others. Big class, big job, but big fun. I can distinctly remember characteristics about several of these students:

Charlie was comical and often wrote about how I was his queen. Riley was always well-dressed, nice, but never did any work. Cordel was the tallest boy in the class. I would often send him to the playground whenever I needed to find someone special and he would usually come back carrying the person in his arms. He was the "Jethro type." Kendra was the smallest, busiest child I had ever seen. She could get her classmates to do just about anything. Sherri was very pretty, always wore her hair in two or three long pigtails, was very athletic, and loved to run. And Carol, I can remember how she would come in crying because she had left her homework at home. She would mess around at her cubby with her book-bag for as long as fifteen minutes on some days. Then all of a sudden she would cry, because she did not want to tell me she had left her homework at home. I never had the heart to fuss at her because she was so sweet and she hadn't meant to leave it home (Besides, Diana had already started softening me up).

Shantay was another sweetie who never gave me any problems. My biggest challenges for that year, I believe, may have been Roco and Carl, both of whom had tempers. Just about anything could send them into a rage. With Carl, I eventually softened him up by channeling his behavior into things he enjoyed doing. He was a fantastic artist and had a perfect handwriting, so I often allowed him to draw in his spare time and for me as well. This seemed to redirect his negative behavior. Roco was another story, I don't know if I ever reached him. Both of these young men could be great students as long as they were not made angry. But through it all, the good and bad times, all of those kids knew that they were loved by their two teachers. This year ended with our class having some of the top readers in the entire first grade. I was really "feeling it". My son was born during this year and I was not nearly as sick during this pregnancy.

Now I know that all of my teaching years thus far sound like they were just glorious. In fact, some were not. Up until this point, most of my children were from inner-city neighborhoods, and some had severe discipline problems. Many never had a parent come up to the school. But these students could be taught just like any other children. I continued to remember my promise – not to ever allow a child to be retained due to behavior. Diana and I showed love on a daily basis and these kids responded to our system.

Shortly after Diana arrived, I learned how to go home on time. She was such a great addition to my program. I often said, "She made me look good" - good enough to be voted "Teacher of the Year". She was truly my inspiration in so many ways - so patient, so sensible, so selfless. Lord, thank You! The Lord truly places angels in our lives and to this day she is still mine.

For the next eight years, we were an unstoppable team. We took pride in being organized, hard workers, and dedicated. Year after year, we produced many successful students. Our first graders usually left prepared for the next grade level. We were often requested by parents and the second grade teachers wished to get our students. Several other changes took place over those years; our classroom count got smaller, we gradually went from thirty students in a classroom to about twenty-two. This was indeed a blessing. The demographics of our classroom also changed. This was due to the completion of the rebuilding of an inner-city school, Creekwood Elementary School. Up until this point, Creekwood Elementary was being rebuilt and all of their students were being bused to Kipling Elementary, so we went from teaching a classroom full of students that qualified for free lunch down to about half that amount. Most of the changes were good, but I wouldn't trade those first few years with my "babies" from the inner-city for anything.

With new demographics, we met more parents. As the years passed, we learned all types of fun ways to teach. We set up centers for every subject. These centers were changed regularly and greatly enhanced learning. Students that come to mind in our earlier groups include Haley, Bridget, Bryant, Raymond, Debbie, Jenny, Sybil, Maurice, Jessica, Larry and Alex. These students were unstoppable. They kept us on our toes. They went further in reading than any other class we had taught. Their parents were also supportive. They donated supplies and time to our classroom. Again, for five years we worked our magic, we took babies and turned them into mature little boys and little girls by the end of each year.

Of course, there were negative influences as well such as the Crack Epidemic. I first learned about crack when one of my first graders told me that she hadn't seen her mother because she was on "the rock". This blew my mind. Communities, especially minority communities, all across the country had been ravaged by this cheap, yet potent drug. Households were being destroyed at an alarming rate, and this crisis had reached my classroom. I couldn't believe it! I no longer had to teach children just their ABCs and 123s, but also coping skills and how to care for themselves when their parents were incapacitated. I had to look for signs of abuse and abandonment in the children's behavior and had to take more seriously my role in nurturing them. This experience made me grow up and realize that what I do on a daily basis is so much more than a job. How could anyone just blindly chase their career and reside in their quiet little bubble when these six year-olds didn't know if they would eat tonight or if their parents would come home at all? In my heart, I wanted to scoop them all up and take them home, be their protector, feed them, and nurture them, but I knew that I couldn't. I could only look for the signs of negative behaviors and be prepared to report it to the authorities. In so, I resolved to do my due diligence if I saw or heard anything to indicate the children were being harmed and to teach my heart out to give them the best education so they can create a different future for themselves; one that didn't include the muck and mire of drug addiction.

Teaching became multi-faceted and presented many challenges. For example, in addition to being a part-time social worker, I also had to teach some parents as well as the kids. Some of the parents, though very few, thought their child could do no wrong. Add that to the fact that we often didn't have the supplies we needed to teach with and we were only paid once a month, some people would begin to wonder if teaching was worth it. However, even with all of that, the good outweighed the bad. More and more I realized that I loved my job and that teaching was truly a blessing.

After Diana and I worked together in first grade for eight years, a Pre-K program was started at our school. We asked to be moved and started our new adventure. Boy, was this different. We went from teaching six and seven year-olds to three and four year-olds. That was a big change. We had to deal with snotty noses, potty training issues, and even children who could barely talk. Of course, 1st graders are young, but they're much more self-sufficient than Pre-K students. This change took some major adjusting, but we were up for the challenge. Along with Pre-K came a brand **new lesson... I needed to learn names fast,** like on day one. Putting a name with a face as soon as possible was important because if you didn't call them by name, those little ones would ignore you. Diana and I had a new room with all types of materials and equipment. We taught, we cooked, we put on plays, we went on field-trips. O-o-o-o-h the trips! There were so many trips! Our kids had fun while learning and we enjoyed teaching them. Now you really had to watch what you said around these little ones. A negative word or phrase, or God forbid, a curse word could easily be repeated. We had to realize that we were receiving these children during their most formative years. So, needless to say, we were careful. But, if there's one thing that can be said about teaching students this young, it's that there's a lot of

LOVE. Preschoolers are some of the most affectionate human beings on the planet. It took little or nothing for a hugging session to take place just out of the blue. Our Pre-K students loved their teachers, and we loved them. And if they thought their teacher needed something, they made it happen. If I mentioned I was hungry, there was Jenny who brought ham wrapped in a paper towel and Stevie who when he heard me say I was "broke" brought me money (which I returned). Cologne and jewelry were snuck out of homes because students wanted their teacher to smell and look good. Boy, did I feel the love! I remember Tamar, Jentay, Donald, Peter, Samantha, Brynn, and London and so many others who came in everyday to get their "learning on". They made most of my five Pre-K years unbelievably rewarding.

During my final school year at Kipling, I think I had my biggest challenge. I had twenty sweet little children. However, about five or maybe six of these sweeties were boys that were spoiled rotten. It was absolutely unbelievable the things that they got away with their parents. **What I didn't know then was that this was just the beginning of the new norm.** For some reason, this year was extremely hard. Every day there was something that at least one of these parents questioned me about. Now even though Diana had softened me up a great deal, I still was a firm believer in discipline. These boys did not have any! Some of these parents seemed to have no parenting skills whatsoever! They actually let their children run them. It was pathetic. We actually had a parent that wanted us to brush her child. Yes that's what I wrote – brush her child, not his hair but him. He was a hyperactive little fellow that really tested my patience to no end. Anyway, his mother told us that brushing him would calm him down and she actually brought us the brush to do it with. I will let you use your imagination to finish this story. By the way, I don't know what ever happened to that brush. A simple rub on the shoulder or pat on the back while talking to him did the job just fine. Quite a few of these boys had mothers that made excuses for their misbehavior. I don't have a problem with parents spoiling kids a little, **but I believe that there is a good spoil and a bad spoil.** And theirs wasn't good!!! **Another lesson learned** here: Let me distinguish the two: "Good spoil" is when parents spoil their children but the children are still respectful and are ok when things don't go their way. In short, good spoil involves kids who are spoiled, but can handle it. "Bad spoil" is the opposite. This is when kids act entitled and are upset when they don't get their way. This school year was trying, but we did our best. And of course, there were also boys and girls in that class that did whatever they could to please their teachers. We worked our usual magic. We just had a few more parent-teacher conferences than usual. But most of our parents still loved and appreciated us.

Another simple **lesson** that can make teaching so much easier is to **get parents on board**. When parents know that you love and know their child, they will do just about anything for you. So, get your parents on board **early.** This teaching endeavor is a joint effort. Teachers can't do it alone. Calling every parent before the year gets going is a tremendous help. Somewhere between the first week of school and Labor Day, I tried my best to learn something about all my students. Then, around the Labor Day weekend, I'd call my parents and open up. I re-introduce myself, tell them about my class procedures, see if they have questions or concerns, and just talk to them about their child. Every parent loves to talk about their child. This really gives a parent the respect and confidence in the teacher needed to make this joint effort a success.

Little did I know that a change was about to come. One morning, while reading the newspaper, I read about an opening in the childcare lab at my alma mater, Jacksonville High School. There were no cell phones allowed in the classroom back then, so I put the paper down and went to the office to use the telephone. I called the principal directly and set up an interview. Long story short, by the end of that school year, I was offered a new position. Excited but scared, I embarked on this journey. There was one (and only one) sad twist, Diana couldn't go with me. My position did not call for a Teacher Assistant. It was so, so hard to part ways. We quickly realized that this only ended our working relationship, but never our friendship.

3

A Lesson In New Beginnings

What can I say? I was so excited. I was going back to my old high school, but now as a teacher! Having attended Jacksonville High from 1973 – 1978, this is where some of my most wonderful days were spent. I never wanted to miss a day of school. I consider those days as some of the happiest of my life, for several reasons. I cheered there, our teachers loved us, I was in the band, I worked in the front office during the school year, I worked with the Track Team, and worked with the Guidance Office during the summer. I practically lived there. I began dating my husband there. Jacksonville High, also known as the Eagles Nest, had truly done a lot to mold me into the person that I had become and here I was, no longer a student, but a faculty member. Having taught elementary school for seventeen years, I didn't know where to start. "What on earth am I going to do with high school students?" I thought..... "Well, I guess I'll teach them."

My new position allowed me to teach high school students how to work with pre-kindergarten students (the best of both worlds). And we actually had a pre-kindergarten lab on campus. My first day was quite interesting and **I learned two lessons immediately. The first lesson was that Elementary and high school are a lot alike**. High school students need some of the same things in a class as elementary students, maybe more. They need rules, consistency, understanding, attention, and love. If you give them these things from the beginning, your program will run much smoother. The end of my first day was quite memorable. Most of that day was spent basically talking and getting to know one another; however, during my last class of the day a young lady knocked on the door and asked to come in and speak to Micah. Assuming they were friends, I allowed her to do so, and within seconds she was fighting him. **The Second high school lesson** (or should I say reminder). **Don't EVER assume anything!!!** From that point on, if someone asked to speak to someone in my class, I asked questions. Things like, "Do you have a pass?"; "Are you all friends?";

and "What do you want with the person?" What a way to be "broken in" on your first day! Security came and my new principal came to make sure I was OK. I assured him I was great! Shortly after that, school was out for the day.

Wow, high school days surely do go by fast. When the bell rang, all the students got up to leave and I asked "Where are you going?" Their response was "to the bus." That's when I realized that I WAS IN LOVE. I realized that I hadn't taken anyone to the bathroom, lunch, or to a bus all day long. What a wonderful surprise!!! At that exact moment, I gained a new respect for teachers at the elementary school level. Aside from that little incident, my day had been much more relaxed than any first day of school I'd ever experienced. This was amazing to me because all I ever did at the elementary level, it seemed, was escort students from one place to another and fix and zip clothes. I was now with young, independent adults. I thought, "Thank You, Lord! I think this is really going to work."

I also received two more surprises that day. I was now a club advisor, which meant I was responsible for advising and preparing students for competitions and fundraising. Also, I was expected to plan and carry out a Pre-K graduation program. Surprise! Surprise!

Surprise! Now these were two surprises that were initially unwelcomed, but I eventually became comfortable handling. The first year I just watched and learned a lot. Well, my job was now to teach high school students how to become teachers. These students would actually work with three to four-year-olds three days per week in a daycare lab setting. I didn't really know where to start, but I kept a journal on everything that I did that first year. This proved to be very helpful in the years to come.

As a class, we only met on Mondays and Fridays because the preschool children came on Tuesdays through Thursday. I started off by giving the high school students writing assignments (which they hated) that were discussed and graded every Monday. Although they weren't fond of the writing assignments, they became routine and helped them become better teachers. First of all, it helped them to feel better about class discussions which made them more comfortable having discussions with the preschoolers. Believe it or not, these sixteen and seventeen-year-olds, supposedly "grown" high-schoolers were very shy around the preschoolers, so my discussions with them helped prepare them to get their preschoolers to speak out. This, in turn, helped expand the language development of the three and four-year-olds. Also, the writing assignments helped me to get to know my students which is extremely important when working with young adults. How can you successfully work with someone if you don't understand them?! Well maybe you can work with them, but understanding them surely does make the process easier. The lessons I learned at Jacksonville! These writing topics, which ranged from stories in the news to thoughts on education, to their being given a chance to share anything else they desired at the end of each assignment taught me a lot. Although a lot of them didn't care to verbally discuss their personal information, they often would write about it. I would read it and always try to give a response either on paper or orally sometime during the week. This they appreciated because they felt they were being heard. And they had a lot to tell! This really helped me to "learn" my students and also led me to another Lesson and one of my famous sayings. **"Learn your students and teach accordingly, because all children cannot be treated or taught the same."** Well the writing assignment was one really great strategy.

Another essential aspect of classroom etiquette that I insisted on was professionalism and showing respect. If we're going to be teachers, we will act like teachers. No cursing, no slang, no incorrect grammar, and address each other by Miss or Mister. This is when I found out that most high school students aim to please. If they know they are loved, most children will try to do whatever is asked of them. These students were used to some serious slang, but not in Ms. Cofer's class. The cursing, loud talking, and rudeness all stopped at the childcare lab! Next came order. Since everyone couldn't be teachers at the same time, groups were organized. There was a teaching group, a planning group, and a clean-up group (kitchen and bath). So, on the lab days when everyone couldn't meet as a class, each group had assigned duties. Order and cleanliness were top priorities. The writing assignments along with discussion; professionalism; and grouping, in addition to a set of well-established rules and guidelines got my first year of high school teaching off to a wonderful start.

There were many teachers and faculty members who advised me. Some were childcare teachers; others were not. There were two great mentors who had been in this same position for years, Ms. Brown and Ms. Williams. I liked their style. Their classroom style and student relationships felt familiar. I was also able to observe Ms. Gaylord and Ms. Walden who were veterans "at the Nest." All of these women taught me how much high school students and elementary students are similar. Ms. Walden was a very capable and intelligent teacher, perhaps the best in the county in her field. I also became fast friends with Mrs. Crenshaw who was that caring office personnel member in the front office who took to the "new kid on the block". She kept me abreast of all due dates on paperwork. And there was also Ms. Abraham who served in the role of bookkeeper. She was simply wonderful at her job. She was instrumental in helping me to keep my classroom and club finances in order. She also had this easygoing personality and disarming sense of humor. This was a great source of calming in the fast pace of high school. By combining my previous experience along with their expertise, I was beginning to feel very comfortable. I also gained some very special lifetime friends. **Lesson learned here: Never be afraid or think you know so much that you can't ask others for help and learn from others.**

Interesting enough, right off the bat, I found myself working with some of the same high-school students that were once my first-grade babies. How cool was that? I had often wondered about how they had turned out. One of the first students that I ran into was Skye. She was in my first class of the day. Skye broke me into the teaching field years earlier. She was this cute little first-grader with thick hair, and she fought almost every day. I am sure I had to spank her a few times during our time together in first grade. Yes, spanking was allowed back then. If only it were allowed today, things might be so much better. Spanking was always the last resort used only if the situation warranted it. I cared enough to pay attention to the child and their behavior. Most children and their parents respected the class rules and behavior issues were resolved on their own without spanking. As for Skye, she had made it through most of high-school and was now a senior in my class. After all that time, our reunion was beautiful. She was still a fighter and had earned much respect from her peers. Luckily for me, she remembered and loved her first-grade teacher. She helped make my transition into high school teaching a little easier. Oddly enough, she also remembered the type of no-nonsense teacher that I was, and gave me much respect. We immediately developed a special bond. Not all of my students were as welcoming as Skye. There were some that were not used to following rules and seemed to want to challenge everything. I just stood fast, prayed, observed, and learned **another lesson… Students act out for a reason and it usually isn't anything personal against the teacher**. This led to another one of my famous sayings that I share with my students and mentees. By the way, I had become mentor for new teachers in the early 90's at the recommendation of Ms. Morris, my principal. This famous saying simply states **"Don't take it personally."** Most students love their teachers and do not mean them any harm. This lesson taught me not to react harshly when students act out. That only adds fuel to the fire. In fact, when we don't react harshly, many times fires can be diffused.

Another **lesson** I learned really early was how to approach a student. **It is best to approach students "one-on-one", not in front of the class.** The latter causes them to want to prove themselves in front of the crowd, but one-on-one is almost always another story. So even my students that met me with much resistance taught me valuable lessons, and I thank them for it. They have made me a better person and teacher. For the most part, my first year at "The Nest" was a pretty good year. There were ups and downs, but one thing I knew for sure was that I was back home to stay.

Over the next nine years, I used my previous experience to train high school juniors and seniors. Year after year, my juniors and seniors eagerly prepared three and four-year olds for kindergarten. Each year I learned more about high school students. As I learned their ways, teaching them became easier. I looked up one day and I had done it. I had made the transition from elementary to high school which, of course, reminds me of another one of Cheryl's famous sayings. **"When you are doing a job that you love, it does not feel like work."** What better job could a person have? The hardest part of my day was actually getting up at 5:00 a.m. so that I could be on time. After arriving at work, my days were fulfilling. Let me say that Jacksonville has always been special to me. There is just something about that school that makes it close to my heart. It gave me a feeling of home, so it would have been really hard for me not to give it my very best. Anyway, for the next nine years or so, I made it my priority to produce students that would become well-trained childcare workers, future teachers, good parents, and just overall productive citizens.

As word spread of all the wonderful things happening in Room 117, my class filled with not only females, but males as well. Also, what better atmosphere for one or two males than a classroom full of females? In fact, it seemed to be more rewarding to see how well the young men worked with the little ones. They also helped keep the drama down among the girls in the class.

As I reflect over my years at "The Nest", fond memories flood my mind. Some of my first memories include my sweet

"Eagle Sister" Sandy who never ever came in with a bad mood. If she did, it was rare! She just didn't seem to let things get the best of her. I am certain that she must have had a bad day every now and then, but it never showed. Even when the girls in my class kept drama going, there was always some problem for me to fix, or an unfinished plan to complete, my Sandy always had a good attitude. Heck, she even helped solve some of my problems.

There was also Ms. Perry, who was in the same class as Sandy and whose writing assignments would always amuse me. She would always include a little slang in her writing assignments and then, neatly in parentheses, write the definition of the slang. She assumed because I didn't allow them to use it verbally, I was unfamiliar with its meaning. She was quite a charmer and kept us laughing, but she always finished her work. This was a nice morning crew.

Another student from my famous morning crew was Richard. Richard was known throughout the school as "out there". If excitement was going on, you'd better believe Richard was somewhere in the middle of it. Some of his teachers absolutely hated to see him coming. That is all his teachers except me. When you put Richard in a classroom full of preschoolers, it was like magic. He loved them and they adored him. As a matter of fact, put him in any area of the lab and he shined. Whenever he had kitchen duty, it was like IHOP; whenever he had bathroom duty, it was spic and span; planning time for him was spent looking for the best activity for his little ones. He was the total package while in the childcare lab. It was as though he went through a metamorphosis. He ran that class. He enjoyed doing it, I enjoyed watching him doing it, and his peers responded well to him. It was a great fit! Richard ended up being the first student from my club that went to competition. He not only won at the local level but also at the state level. His name later went on a plaque for T.O.Y (Teacher of the Year) which remains in class for all to see. Right about now, I'm feeling like the old lady who lives in a shoe, and I haven't even told you about half of my children. Richard taught me a **lesson; he liked to run things and I let him. He was given choices within my "choice range"**. It worked for both of us. His wild personality along with my rather reserved one could have been a horrible mix. We found a medium that created success for both of us. Teachers don't have to get all caught up on showing students who's the boss. The rules determine who's in charge and teachers don't have to "act" like they are in charge to actually "be in charge". When a student doesn't respond properly to the rules, following-through with the consequences is often all it takes. However, it is important to establish the rules AND the consequences on DAY ONE and following-through with them. Sometimes these consequences are uncomfortable and time consuming for the teacher as well, but necessary.

Other names that come to mind from my first period classes include JC, Olivia, Mitchell, Gidget and Briana Ball. These students and so many others helped to contribute to very successful morning crews throughout the years.

In stark contrast to first period were my third and fourth period classes. Every year they were my wild classes. They always seemed to be the classes that were wide awake. First and second periods were always so early that the students seemed calm, quiet and sleepy, but third and fourth periods (a.k.a. the lunch crew) were held during the time of day when everyone was awake. These wide-awake students would make the special lunches for the babies or do extra special outside activities with them. They would literally wear the kids out and then put them down for nap. Year after year, I had to find ways to channel all that energy into a productive way of working with the little ones.

Margo, Martha, Tasha, Batina, and Connie immediately come to mind as I recall my third period class from my early days at Jacksonville. Margo and Martha absolutely adored their preschoolers. Tasha was moody and spoiled; Connie was conscientious; and Batina was loud and had a beautiful handwriting. But when you put these young ladies in the Pre-k lab, they took care of business. Connie and I still keep in touch to this day. Batina and I had a rough start; however, by the time she enrolled in the second semester of the childcare class, we were inseparable. **Lesson learned: Never give up on your students.**

As I mentioned, Batina and I had a very, very rough start. For example, I met her in the hallway during breakfast one morning and she cursed out loud. I corrected her about it, and she told me I wasn't her mother. I tried to explain to her that I was fully aware of that fact and that her mother needed to tell her that ladies don't use that kind of language. She wasn't interested in what I had to say. She didn't like me from there on out, and now she's in my class. I knew that she probably wasn't going to transfer to another class, so I needed to find a way to make this work. Consistently, I gave her opportunities to participate in things that she did well. She had great penmanship and LOTS of energy. These two attributes are exactly what is needed to teach small children writing skills and keep up with their high energy level. Whenever I observed Batina positively using these skills, I would encourage her. Not immediately, but eventually that encouragement made a difference in our teacher-student relationship. In fact, by her second year in my class she could run the lab by herself. Boy how she had grown.

Another student from first grade that I soon came in contact with was Riley who was in my 3rd period. He didn't remember me at first, but as soon as I saw him and heard his name, I knew exactly who he was. When Riley was in my first-grade class, he was a playful fellow who was extremely well dressed. He was smart, but didn't get much work finished. He was almost never able to go to recess because he was always inside catching up on his class work. He was also playful, so he was on the receiving end of serious discipline. Now a senior in high school, he had not changed much. I was really hoping that he had good memories of me. To my surprise he had none, at least not at first. After a few days of our reunion and questioning, it hit him. All of a sudden he said "I remember you. Why didn't you ever let me go to recess?" We had a laugh because he knew exactly why he never went. Well, that question led to another, then another, and more laughter. Riley had not changed much at all! Still very friendly, well-dressed, smart, and playful. Everyone loved him. He was very pleasant to be around and the pre-schoolers loved to have him as their teacher. We had an absolutely wonderful teacher-student relationship. He was comfortable with me and I with him. Riley once told me, "You know, Mrs. Cofer, you can take the teacher out of the ghetto, but you can't take the ghetto out of the teacher." He did not mean anything negative at all by this. It meant he loved me and he felt comfortable and knew I loved him back. He wasn't being rude and never ever, ever, ever showed disrespect. Riley graduated in 2004 and he still keeps in touch. About every two or three months, he and Andrew, his best friend, give me a call on 3-way.

Andrew was another child I inherited. He came to me as a wild junior and I actually wanted him out of my class, but once I found out how to use his wild behavior for "good", it was like magic. He was also a fantastic teacher because of his energy and outgoing personality. He ended up enrolling in my class that year and ultimately enrolled in my advanced class. During the second year in my class, Andrew absolutely ran the entire operation. Mondays and Fridays were the days when the preschoolers weren't there and I would always start our two-hour block with writing and discussion.

We had writing and discussion on Monday and weekly review on Friday. The year Andrew was there, I sat back and observed. On Mondays, he would start off reading what he had written and commence to call on his classmates, and boy was he raw (respectively raw). He would have us absolutely rolling. He didn't know it, but this actually made the others want to read what they had written. On Fridays, he would go to each group and tell them what they had done well during the week in the preschool lab and also on what they needed to improve. The amazing thing about this was that his peers respected and listened to him. They never got mad at him for giving his weekly "suggestions". Rather, they would discuss it and move on. Their genuine love and respect for each other was incredible. These kids took care of their teacher in more ways than one - Having graduated in 2005, Andrew has held the same job since graduation. Andrew and Riley are truly "my boys". I can count on hearing from one or both of them at least once a month. I am proud of these two very hard-working young men.

Other students also come to mind as I think about some of my end-of-the-day classes. One was like a super student who always had her assignments, came to class on time, was always prepared, and was a heck of a well-organized little teacher. She was in my last class of the day and often gave me encouragement, support, and a feeling of worth (indirectly). This young lady ended up becoming a teacher. In that same class, however, was a student that only came to class once or twice per week and she never seemed to care much about class assignments. Even though she never did any assignments, she had all intentions of graduating and she needed my class to do so. This was unfortunate for both of us. Unfortunate for me because I did not realize that she needed this class for graduation and unfortunate for her because I was not the confrontational type and she "actually" thought that she didn't have to do the work and that it would somehow "work itself out" to her advantage. She, too, taught me a **valuable lesson. From that day forward, I asked my students on "day one" specific questions – such as, "Are you a senior?", " Do you need this class to graduate?", and "May I have your parent's telephone number?"** I was determined the students got special reminders all year about graduation requirements. Did that take a lot of effort! This situation reminds me of an **earlier lesson. Don't assume their parents are aware, don't assume that the student and parents aren't both in denial.**

Some of the most important lessons I learned came from students who weren't excited about being in my class. For every student that comes into your classroom and excels, you can believe there will be another that doesn't want to be there and won't commit themselves to the work. I encountered this type of student often. Some had trouble dealing with the three and four-year olds that they were supposed to care for and others had trouble just dealing with me. When considering this two other students come to mind, Mickey and TaQuoya. After a few days of my drilling and a classroom of three and four-year olds, they were ready to leave and withdraw from my class. I can distinctly remember these two students coming to me and saying, "I've got to get out of here!" However, somehow I convinced both of them to stay and they actually ended up enjoying and excelling in the class. Go figure.

I can't let this chapter end without mentioning three other students that are truly special to me. I'll start with the two siblings, Olivia and Don. Each of them gave me a unique experience. Olivia was that student that came into the classroom with this serious, almost mean look on her face. A look that rarely seemed to change. However, her look was not a representation of her actual personality. She was anything but mean. I learned that behind that mean look was such a a kind and loving spirit. In fact, she was one of the sweetest and most cooperative students I've taught. Her brother Don, had that same loving spirit. Don was a remarkably gifted athlete who excelled at all sports, but he was just an amazing football player. He made headlines literally every week, and I couldn't have been prouder. We became close almost instantly, and I looked upon him as another of my "sons." Which leads me to my other child, Martha. She too was an outstanding athlete. Fierce on the basketball court and feared by her competitors. It was amazing to see both of these athletes transform from their rough competitive exteriors into these warm, loving teachers that were adored by their prekindergarten students.

Although I taught hundreds of students, the ones that stick out either taught me valuable lessons or seem to be the ones with a genuine love for children and teaching them. Now there are so many outstanding students that took my class, far too many to recall, however, more will be discussed in later chapters.

4

A Lesson In Solidarity

Throughout all of my years teaching high school, I seemed to draw students that became "my children", at least while we were in school. I would also seem to get hooked on students that had a genuine love for little children. However, there was another type of high school student that would always get me hooked. This was the student that also had that genuine love for children, but who was also "raw". What you saw was what you got!

Shortly after arriving at Jacksonville, I began meeting students who were "raw". These students were those who had been through some things, weren't trying to be raw, but were because of the hand that life had dealt them. I truly believe that these students taught me my greatest lessons. They made me see life from a prospective that I had never thought about before.

After being at Jacksonville for a couple of years, we inherited a new Assistant Principal, Mr. Tate. I met most of these raw students due to the efforts of Mr. Tate. He was loud and firm, but he cared about those students. I didn't know him personally but he knew most of my family, so we hit it off right away. Immediately, he started enrolling students into my class that he felt needed just a little more supervision, discipline, and consistency. Why me? I don't know, I guess I was just lucky.

When considering this, two students immediately come to mind. One of the first students that I inherited from this assistant principal was Jenny. She was a 4'9" fireball. She would fight you if she thought that you were even looking at her. She even got stabbed once. She came to class with her hard exterior, and I immediately knew I could not handle her in the same manner as I handled my calmer students. She was loud, full of laughter, and full of play, but she was smart and she loved kids, so I sat back and observed. I made it my business to capitalize on her positive qualities and to channel her not-so-positive qualities in helping the preschoolers.

Over the course of about two years, she stopped fighting so much. She used up all of the loud and wild energy to plan and create the best lessons and keep our preschoolers well-engaged. She ended up being one of my best teachers. The preschoolers absolutely adored her. Not only did she do a great job teaching preschoolers, but eventually became the perfect role model for them as well. She taught me so much. Underneath all the rage was a little girl who never really wanted to fight but always felt she had to do so. The oldest of four siblings, she always had to be the big sister and fight for her siblings. This was because many times there weren't any adults around. She had been given an adult role at such a young age, and she was only doing what she knew to do. These experiences taught her to be "super strong". It took a while because it was so hard for her to trust in others.; however, I eventually gained her trust. No matter how angry she became, I continued to show her unconditional love. She finally realized that there was nothing that she could ever do to make me stop loving her. The **first lesson** that Jenny reminded me of or taught me **is that when people act out, it is not personal but it is usually for a reason: usually fear or frustration**. Children do it and adults do it too.

Students today have so many distractions and reasons to worry, many of which are things that I never even thought about when I was their age. Moreover, sometimes a teacher or a fellow student can say the one thing to trigger a flashback, causing an explosion. It is how we react to a situation that determines the outcome. Not reacting harshly to these situations can totally deflate the entire outcome. It's hard to argue and be mad in an argument all by yourself. The next **lesson** Jenny taught me/reminded of is that **respect is earned**. This young lady came to me as a discipline problem. I never argued with her or demanded her to respect me. I just gave her my love and respect through my actions, and I gained her respect naturally without struggle and without having to ask. This young lady gave me strength because she was such a hard fighter and she wasn't trying to impress anyone. Jenny was trying to survive and was just raw. I love her so much! Not only did she learn how to stop fighting, but her biggest lesson may have been to use her wild behavior in a positive manner.

Jenny has grown up to become a sensible, calm young lady. This didn't happen overnight though. I've had to go pick Jenny up many times and calm her down after receiving frantic phone calls from her. She is currently working and has been doing so for some time now. She completed management training and left those fighting days behind her. She graduated from Jacksonville in 2006 and we still remain close. She's my Jenny Mae. I am s-o-o proud of her. I could go on and on about her. To tell you the truth, her entire story would be a whole "notha" book. Both Jenny and her sister still keep in contact with me regularly.

Another "raw" student who was placed in my class because Mr. Tate felt he needed guidance was Charlie Smith. Charlie came into my class and I immediately said to myself, "I'm going to kill Mr. Tate." This boy was a clown! School work was the farthest thing from his mind. Every time he came in he started social hour, or at least he tried. Whenever I was not going over my usual beginning of the year information, Charlie would chime in with his humor to get the class going. Now, I like to have fun just as much as anyone else, but I am serious about my work and I do believe that there's a time and place for fun and games. On the other hand, I knew two things for sure: (1) Mr. Tate placed him in my class and he wasn't going anywhere; (2) Mr. Tate felt I could break through to this kid. So instead of "going off" on the clown, I observed and planned my strategy.

After about three days of observing and strategic planning, I pulled Charlie aside after class and informed him that I had assigned him to detention because I was determined not to let him fail this class due to his behavior. In the first three days, little of his work had been completed due to his distracting himself and others. Therefore, he had to come after school and catch up. I didn't make it sound like I was fussing, but only that here's a second chance to get your work done. I really didn't think he'd come, but it was worth a try. I figured if he did, that would give me a chance to talk to him one-on-one and possibly understand him a little better.

Well, as luck would have it as soon as it was time for detention, my principal called a faculty meeting. I left his class assignment with another student just in case he showed up. This student informed me that he knew Charlie and further confirmed that he probably would not show. Long story short – I went to the faculty meeting and when I got back, the assignment that I had left had been completed. Charlie had come, completed his class assignment, and had gone. My student and I were both stunned! My strategic plan was now in motion. I could not wait to praise him the following morning. Did he beam when I did! This was the beginning of a very serious bond.

Nonetheless, Charlie started getting serious about my class and had the preschoolers absolutely in love with "Mr. Smith". He ran that lab. Contrary to the classroom Charlie Smith, the outside Charlie was "Gangsta" with a capital "G". If I didn't know before what the students meant by "gangsta" or "G" now I did. Very popular and well respected on the outside but in the childcare lab, he was gentle and very concerned about "his babies". He represented our class during homecoming as "Mr. Childcare" and he took this title very seriously? After he was voted Mr. Childcare, that was all he wanted to be referred to as for a while. He represented us well, and man could he cook! Since our lab had a kitchen, we would often fix special treats for the preschoolers. Charlie would bring all kinds of food, including steak to treat his favorite teacher and students. The meals were s-o-o-o-o tasty. Charlie continued to take my class for two years and became an excellent student/teacher/son. Now don't get me wrong; Charlie was no angel and I did not agree with everything he did, but one thing I knew for sure was he would never tell me a lie (good or bad) and he could be trusted.

Charlie once made a profound statement, saying that "We are all just products of our environment." So innocent and simple, but true. A person can only do as well as what they "know to do." The hand that life dealt Charlie was not fair, but boy did he do well with what he had. Since I met him in 2004, he has indeed been one of my most trusting, caring, and loyal friends and to this day he still calls me mother. He graduated in 2006 and calls me quite often, never missing Mother's Day. The **lesson** Charlie taught me… **Once you gain the respect of that popular loud child who loves to be a distraction, you automatically gain the respect of those students that look up to him.** Once I won Charlie's love and respect, his audience followed quickly. (Go ahead; act a fool if you want to with this type of student and you will probably regret it!)

Please note, BY NO MEANS did I allow Charlie to run my class. I simply treated him in such a respectable manner that he couldn't help but feel love and return it. Even though Charlie could be a class clown, he was definitely a leader and I do mean LEADER in a positive big way where his friends respected and followed his lead. Once students found out how Charlie felt about "Mrs. Cofer", Mrs. Cofer was cool and I'm not just talking about the students in my class. I'm also referring to other students throughout the entire building. Another lesson he taught me: **Even "gangstas" respond positively when shown encouragement and unconditional love. Also, it is so much easier to be nice than to fuss all the time.**

5

A Lesson In Unconditional Love (Just like Mine)

During the 2002-2003 school year, the Lord brought two more very special students into my life. At that time, even I did not realize just how special they would become. I can't explain it, but sometimes I feel as though I could have actually given birth to them. We grew so close. Listen as I tell you our story and maybe you will see why I feel like these two students are just like my own. I will begin with Stella whom I met when she was in the tenth grade. She took my class third period. Right away she seemed different and was one of those students who only had to be given directions once. She never left a task undone and if she started an assignment on Monday and just happened to be absent on Tuesday and Wednesday, as soon as she arrived on Thursday she would pick up right where she left off. She always followed through with whatever she started.

Perhaps this does not sound like anything special as she was only doing what she was supposed to be doing. However, this is rarely seen in students in high-school. In fact, some adults have a hard time finishing what they start. Stella was a star student from day one! Not only was she good with her academic skills, but she also knew something about showing initiative. She would rarely be found sitting idle with nothing to do. Whenever she wasn't teaching our preschoolers or doing work from our textbook, she was busy preparing for her next session with the preschoolers. She might even be studying for another class. This young lady knew how to make good use of her spare time. Of course, she was an honor student. She was my type, the kind of student that made a teacher's job EASY! I quickly inherited her as my child. She became a welcome presence in my home and among my family.

During her junior year, she did not take the second part of my class; however, she did remain in my club and planned to go to competition with us. Unfortunately, both of her parents passed within months of each other during her junior year. What a devastating blow!! Here she was only sixteen years old, with no close relatives nearby. How in the world would she handle this? Well, she handled this tragedy with such poise and strength.

Upon returning to school after each death, she immediately regained focus on her classwork and was chosen as a hostess during the senior graduation services, an honor offered only to our top juniors. Stella and I became very close during her grieving period, and our relationship evolved into a mother-daughter relationship. During this time my son Reggie began attending Jacksonville High School. Since they were both Juniors and both enrolled in many of the same classes, they became friends fast. Before I knew it, they had a mutual respect and considered each other to be like brother and sister. She eventually became a very significant part of our family.

That next year, Stella teamed up with Lisa, another very conscientious young lady. I placed these two young ladies in the same group. Both of them could run the childcare lab alone and they were both an absolute joy. These girls teamed up for competition that year and won our chapter a first place award regionally and a trip to state competition. But back to Stella. It seemed that whatever she participated in was bound for success. She went on that year to be one of Mrs. Cofer's "High School Teachers of the Year". She graduated, qualified for the Hope Scholarship, and went on to graduate from Georgia Southern University majoring in Early Childhood Education.

Stella's experiences and/or ordeals **taught me how to be strong in the face of adversity.** Although I am much older, I don't know if I could hold it together as well as she has. To this day, we remain in constant contact. I believe that out of all my children, she is probably the moodiest, but she is also the most driven and most mature. On April 1st of her junior year in college she sent me a long text message saying how sorry she was and that she knew I expected more from her, but she was pregnant! Of course, I texted her right back to say "April Fool!" I was certain this was a joke, but it was not and Shayna, her daughter, was born later that year. Stella finished school, received a Bachelor Degree and Master's Degree and is working on her Specialist Degree. She is also happily married. School would have been the first thing to go for most people, but she's like superwoman. I am certain there will continue to be good things in store for this awesome young lady.

I met my other special child, D'Waun, during that same year, and he took my class first period. He was another one of those "raw" students. This young man walked into my classroom with the word attitude written all over his face, heck all over his body. Immediately, I said to myself, "Why do they keep putting these young men in a childcare class? They don't want to be here and I am not that happy about having them here." Nonetheless, I would do my usual spill. Starting with my icebreakers, I try to get everyone to open up. This young man gave me no reaction. He sat there with one of the meanest expressions a person could imagine. This happened for a couple of days. Finally, on day three of that school year, I called specifically on him in class. Oh my Goodness, why on earth did I do that? It definitely got a response out of him. He immediately told me what he was not going to do and to leave him alone! Several questions flooded my mind. Now I'm saying to myself, "What had I said to make a kid act this way? How in the heck can I get him out of this class? Should I act a fool because he did?" Well, I did make a little smart remark and I moved on to the next student. Time eased on and things didn't get better right away. This young man came in most mornings with the same mean look and usually put his head down. After a while, he would pick and choose assignments that he would take part in. Remarkably enough, these assignments, though not consistent, were done well. So, I realized that the student either liked writing or had a lot to share. I'd pay close attention to these assignments and give one-on-one positive feedback sometimes during the week. Gradually, he seemed to feel comfortable doing most lab day assignments and even started writing intriguing information during our Monday writing assignments.

One day, during one of our writing assignments, he wrote about visiting his mother – at her grave. Those questions that I had asked myself earlier in the year were now answered. This had to be the reason that this child acts and looks so mean. Those questions were answered, but now I had an entire set of new questions. What could have happened? When? Why? How can I help him? Of course, I could not ask him any of these questions, but I knew that this great loss had to be the root of his demeanor. Right then and there, I realized there was no way for me to handle this student the same way as a child who still had their mother. Before, when he was distant, I would be also. I decided to show warmth with this child because I could only imagine what it was like for him to be without a mother. I was 40+ and I couldn't imagine being without my mother at my age. As I warmed up, something amazing happened, he also warmed up. Before I knew it, I managed to get a smile out of him. What a gorgeous smile! A neat handwriting and consistent work patterns finally emerged. He continued to be very reserved and often displayed that mean look, but I felt that I was breaking ground. That is until he had to leave.

One afternoon out of the blue, D'Waun paid a visit to my class outside of normal hours. He informed me that he would be leaving to go to alternative school and he had walked over to my classroom (from the other side of campus) only to tell me goodbye. Imagine my surprise. He explained that he had been accused of something that he had not done and he wanted me to know that he was innocent. He also told me that he would not be coming back after serving his time at the alternative school. Now this coming from any other student probably would have had an entirely different meaning, but this visit in the middle of the day, on the opposite side of the school campus, to tell me that he cared what I thought meant that he loved me and he knew I loved him too. I informed him of how sorry I was for his misfortune and how pleased and surprised I was that he came all the way to tell me goodbye. It was not until that very moment that I knew I had broken through. Too bad he was leaving.

At that moment I saw a totally different young man. I saw a gentle, kind, caring, sweet, innocent child. He almost seemed scared. I assured him that I would check on him while he was at the alternative school, and I did. **Lesson I'm reminded of here:**

Learn your students; teach them, accordingly, and treat them with unconditional love.

And visit D'Waun is exactly what I did. During that time my sister was a teacher at the alternative school. Not only did she keep a close watch on him, but whenever I stopped to see her, I would go by and check on him. Boy, did he smile whenever I visited. Before we knew it, his time had been served and the year was over. Well, who do you think walked into my room on the very first day of school at the beginning of the next school year. Yes, the young man that said he would not be coming back to Jacksonville was back. He was back and wanted to finish the coursework he had not been able to complete before he went to the alternative school. Upon entering this time when he came into the classroom, he wore a beautiful smile and felt comfortable. Over the course of one year, I watched a shy little boy emerge into a confident, dependable young man. His frown changed to a smile. His rough edge softened up. His in-class naps evolved into consistent work habits. His relaxed attitude transformed to a warm person who seemed to care about those around him, and man could he work. He had initiative, my absolute favorite word, and the first word that I taught each of my classes. In fact, I am certain that if you were to ask students that came through

Room 117, "What is Mrs. Cofer's favorite word?", without hesitation they would tell you "Initiative". As a matter of fact, one of the several most rewarding moments I experienced was when one of my former students (Don) went off to college and came back to tell me that one of the first things his college professor asked was to give a definition of initiative. He was one of the few students that knew. Showing initiative is so important. Yet, very few young adults ever show any or know what it means. D'Waun had initiative. All I had to do was show or tell him something one time, and it was done. I was "his teacher" and everyone knew it.

Upon returning to Jacksonville, D'Waun began performing better, even in other classes, due to the confidence he felt in my class. I had actually helped change this child's demeanor by changing mine. Oh, praise God! How different this could have turned out. Here was a motherless child who had every reason in the world to act out; be mean, break laws, and even do drugs. Instead, he had become a role model for others.

After completing both part one and part two of the childcare classes, D'Waun remained in the club I advised and during his senior year served as Vice President! Can you believe that? Not only did he serve as an officer, he also VOLUNTEERED to attend competition where students selected an area to compete in involving some type of "speaking" in front of a group. When he first informed me of his desire to attend competition, I thought he was joking, because even though he had changed a lot, he still wasn't really a big talker. So you can imagine how stunned, yet overjoyed, I was when he volunteered to go. Along with Omar, another one of my school "children," D'Waun selected the topic "The High School Drop-Out Rate", and they worked diligently on their project, practiced speaking, purchased nice suits, went to competition, and won one of the two top places in our region. This landed them in the position to be invited to compete at the state level. This was their first time competing and they won! By now, I was beginning to believe that D'Waun was my good luck charm.

I need to say a little more about Omar. He was an immensely intelligent young man who exhibited such creativity, ingenuity, and personality. I so enjoyed teaching him. I often jested with him that if he'd only use his powers for good and not evil, that he could accomplish so much. Because unfortunately, Omar could often be led astray or let the allure of negative dealings distract him from his studies. When he was entirely focused, he was simply brilliant. Omar has since grown considerably, and is realizing his true potential. He always reminds me of those words I would say to him and regularly tells me that he is now using his intelligence for good.

Well, back to the competition, not only did they win, but for the first time ever since I began teaching high school and became a club sponsor, I took ten students to regional competition. Four of them were young, handsome, well-behaved, intelligent young men, and six were beautiful, intelligent, young ladies.

When we walked into the building, we captured everyone's attention. We were like a team, maybe even family. We were well-groomed, mannerable, and had that Jacksonville spirit and pride. What else could we do but win? Each one of them placed first or second, high enough for each student to advance to state competition. We were off to state competition! I called this group "My Big Ten". After I finally got the hang of what competition was all about, my club flourished.

As time passed, D'Waun became an ideal student. He graduated from high school and attended college for a while. I met his family and he met mine. We all fell in love with him, and he with us. To this day, we still consider each other family. Now he works, owns his own home, and is still a very nice calm young man. We talk quite often. This story could have ended so differently. **Lesson here: Just be nice. Kindness can go such a long way.**

I thank God for giving me the wisdom to turn the other cheek. Even when D'Waun gave me much attitude, I did everything I could to show kindness. Over time, my kindness changed his heart. What better way for a teacher to teach than by her actions? This experience also reminded me of a **former lesson: "Don't take anything personally."** Often when teenagers act out, it is usually nothing against the teacher. They are simply, as they put it, "going through something." D'Waun has grown up to be a successful and productive citizen. He has been on the same job for several years and is the best father ever to the love of his life, his baby Jalynn.

6

A Lesson in Celebration

The year was 2003-2004 and I seemed to be on a roll. I had finally established myself as a well-organized, veteran high school teacher. I had it down to a science. That first month or so I would work my butt off, consistently going over class routines, testing students over the routine, and practicing the routine over and over and over. After the first month of hard training, the rest of the year was a breeze as the class almost ran itself. Students around "The Nest" knew "Mrs. Cofer". I was one of those teachers that most students felt comfortable being around. All of my classes that year seemed to be on top of their game. Our club was quite productive and our daycare was full. Quite a change from that first year when I only averaged about eight preschoolers. We even had a waiting list.

I was especially excited that year because I had a larger than usual advanced class. The advanced class came to me the last period of the day and was filled with students that actually wanted to take my class again for a second dose of my madness. Well, that year the class was fifteen strong and was filled with students that no longer needed that first month of extensive training. They were already in "Cofer Mode", and boy did they make life grand. They already knew my thoughts, understood me, knew how I wanted things done, AND they still loved me. I referred to them as my family, my breath of fresh air. They were indeed like sisters and brothers, and to this day whenever I see any of them, they ask about other members of that class. They absolutely ran that lab. Before I could think of telling them what to do, it was already done. They were divided into three groups and all of the groups were outstanding. Boy, oh boy was life good. Andrew, Lexie, Netra, Shantese, Cooney, Booner, Nikki, Truman, and of course, D'Waun quickly come to mind when I think of that wonderful class. These kids took care of their teacher and they took care of business. I cannot end this chapter without mentioning that I gained a godson from this class; Mr. Truman, an outstanding student that transferred from Jersey. He served as President of the club I advised. He was mature beyond his years and made my job as Advisor so much easier. He was baptized during that year and asked me to be his Godmother. I was honored. We still keep in touch and now he is a hard-working husband and father of three.

It was hypnotizing to watch those students run that room. Other teachers were amazed, parents were amazed, and even I was amazed! To top things off, that year my co-workers thought enough of me to allow me to represent Jacksonville as Teacher of the Year. This means that I had been voted Teacher of the Year twice in my career; once at both schools where I taught – on the elementary and high school levels. Imagine that. What an honor! This really made me feel loved.

There were many great teachers at Jacksonville and many who had been there a lot longer than me, but for some reason, I was chosen. I think my kindness, combined with my genuine ability to get through to and along so well with others, played a larger role in my selection as Teacher of the Year than my actual teaching. I don't mean to slight myself and I truly appreciated the honor, but I also know that I was well loved and respected by peer teachers. What a Great Feeling!!!! This made them want to vote for me. I looked up one day and I was Teacher of the Year again! Thank you students for being so great that you make me look good, and thank you co-workers for your votes of confidence. Boy did I feel the love!

7

A Lesson In Accountability

I cannot go any further without mentioning AYP. AYP stands for Adequate Yearly Progress and is a process that includes testing students in four or five different academic areas. If the students fail, even after passing all classes for 12 years, they DO NOT graduate. The schools across our country have gone "test crazy" in order to meet AYP. It seems as though all the administrators think about is AYP and data. Today's students are not getting a fair take on life. The morals and social skills that used to be taught by parents in the home are no longer being taught. These skills must be taught in the school in order to get the desired results for AYP. Households have changed so much over the last two to three decades, especially in the inner city. Two-parent households are almost extinct. Our children are exposed to things in society that we were never exposed to when we were their age, or even when my children were their age. They have been left to fend for themselves. They are surrounded by crime, drugs, constant fighting, and violence. Often, there is no sense of security, housing isn't consistent, and those with housing are often without electricity or water. So sad. It's sad when a child cuts on a light switch and immediately thinks that the power bill hasn't been paid, instead of thinking maybe it might need a light bulb. So sad that parents curse children and belittle them so much that they actually begin to feel worthless. So sad that a child feels responsible for not having food to eat or socks to wear. Even sadder that on the coldest school day of the year, a child has on no socks, but is so immune to the cold that his/her feet are not even cold. How can you meet AYP when you haven't had anything to E-A-T?!?! Our system's priorities are in the wrong place. There is no doubt that we need to make AYP, but first we must figure out how to reach these kids that come from such troubled backgrounds.

There is no way I'll ever believe that the same teaching techniques should be used for every child. Don't misunderstand what I'm saying. All students can be taught and can learn, but different students require different techniques. A lot of the children that I had the "privilege" of working with were no doubt from underprivileged homes. They needed me and I "darn shole" needed them. Things with them were not always as they seemed. They were remarkable at putting the best on the outside. For a lot of my students, school was the only normalcy they ever had. Some of my students, my babies, were victims of all types of abuse. Some of the abuse was intentional, while some was not. Some parents were not able to do any better. Many high school students had to not only take care of themselves and their siblings, but their parents as well. How can this type of student possibly be rated the same way that a student from a normal household is rated? There is no way. It's not fair!!! Someone has dropped the ball and our students deserve better. School boards are always making cuts. All this does is cut someone out of an education. Instead of making cuts – cutting teachers, assistant principals, nurses, etc., school boards need to find a way to put more people in schools. They are wearing out the staff that is left. How can we reach students with all of the budget cuts with funding? When we do get money, there's always a clause about how to use the money. The teacher can never use it as she sees fit. Our inner-city schools need so much but are given so little and teachers are still expected to make things happen. So unfair – no resources with added responsibility. This, in addition to students that are full of rage, equals frustrated teachers and a school full of potential drop-outs. Well maybe not a school full, but the possibility of increasing the drop-out rate. Oh, how I wish there was a way to help our students not only educationally, but socially and morally.

Now there are many students that can handle the not so normal situations, and they thrive and do well in school. They show respect and they seem to function as productive students, but what about the ones that can't handle these circumstances? Everyone can't do it. What about the ones who have such a hard time dealing with their personal situations that they make it hard for everyone else to learn? They rarely show respect to their peers or teachers. Often they start altercations and disrupt the entire day. And, what can I say? Let's not forget these group of kids are not low income, but feel so privileged that they come off as disrespectful.

Can someone please tell me how to handle children that always talk back, that walk out while you are talking to them, that get in your face as if they are ready to fight? How can these children be taught to meet AYP without teaching them first how to behave and listen? It can be done, but not with budget cuts. Yes, I agree that these students can learn, but other steps must be taken before we can ever meet AYP.

After several years of AYP and thousands of students not receiving diplomas, the AYP rule changed. Now what?????

I can't speak for other counties, but at least in our county changes are being made. It is so refreshing to see new initiatives that consider the whole child, including their background and environment. Several new programs are being implemented right here in our county. A definite move in the right direction. Thank you Lord!!!!!!

8

A Lesson In Change

Well...... back to my story. I couldn't believe it! I was about to start my twenty-seventh year teaching at my old high school. Where had the time gone? Boy did the years fly by and how much fun I had! I can truly say that I hadn't felt like I had gone to work in ages. Rather, I felt like I had gotten up every morning, "hung out" with young adults, and taught some serious lessons. I loved my job and I loved my babies.

That year would be different. For the first time since arriving at Jacksonville, there were two teachers in my classroom and this made my load a little lighter because there was a teacher on the high school side and one on the Pre-K side. In the past, I had done both with the help of my high schoolers. Now I could concentrate on my high school students and spend more time with them.

Instead of three classes that lasted two hours each, I now had four classes and they had more students than usual. I was a little anxious about this at first because my room was so small, but after my rules, regulations, and routines were established and understood by everyone, the year kicked off without incident. Within weeks I had mesmerized another group of young adults. I was feeling the love and so were they. This was also my first year ever teaching ninth-graders, and boy did they pile them in my class. They turned out to be the easiest ones to train. They had never been to high school before, so they didn't know what to expect and easily conformed to my rules. We were crowded, but we made it work. We also had a new principal that year, so things were just new all the way around.

As I stated earlier, the first day of school usually made me feel uneasy, whether with four-year olds or sixteen-year olds, but all of this was behind me and year twenty-seven was off to what I felt was a grand beginning. My club was up and running and, by now it was one of the most popular clubs in the building. Officers had been elected and events for the year were being planned. I even had an abstinence group up and running. For the first time since I started this group, I actually had young men come and ask to join. Life was grand.

One day as I walked in the house after work during the first few weeks of school, my telephone rang. There was this familiar voice offering me an Instructional Coach position at another school. Boy did I not see that coming. Well I guess I need to explain. The previous summer I applied for an Instructional Coach position posted on the Board of Education's website. It sounded like an interesting position and it only required me to have a Master Degree. The deadlines for the application came and went.

Towards the end of July, I received a call for an interview for a position at a high school in the south part of town. However, having always been an inner-city type girl, the position really didn't faze me, so I didn't accept the position and went on with business as usual. It was near the end of August when I received a call from Mrs. Teasley, my former Assistant Principal, who offered me the Instructional Coach position at an inner-city elementary school about two minutes away from Jacksonville High. I thought, "Ain't the Lord somebody?!? This is why I didn't pursue the first offer". I didn't know what to do with myself! My first response was to burst into laughter. I was shocked! Then I asked Mrs. Teasley to give me a minute, or better yet, a few days to decide. I was torn. My year was off to a great start, I had fallen for my students once again, and they were feeling me. I knew my job and I had made teaching the childcare class a work of art. It was fun, and I was productive. On the other hand, here was an opportunity for a slight promotion, working with a principal who had taught me so much in the past. No more lesson plans would have to be written and no more papers would have to be graded. There would be a later work schedule and a chance to work on all levels in an elementary school. My only concerns were how long the position would be around and how long the principal would be around. What shall I do?!?

9

A Lesson In Destiny

Well, needless to say, I took Mrs. Teasley up on her offer to become an Instructional Coach. It was late September before all of the transfer paperwork was done and replacement for my class was found. I walked into Creekwood Elementary School and saw little people running down the hall, and I said to myself "What in the world have I done?" I had actually forgotten how busy elementary kids were. Thank God I was not in a classroom with these little ones all day. This was truly a culture shock after being in high school for close to ten years. I spent most days going in and out of different classrooms trying to observe and assist where needed and doing the many things an Instructional Coach does.

One very interesting thing that happened while at Creekwood was that I was now coming in contact with the children of the students I taught at the beginning of my career in the 80's. What a wonderful reunion! I was especially excited to see Carl, my little first grader that I loved s-o-o much. I reunited with many other students and just enjoyed seeing what they grew up to be. Outside of that, I honestly missed having my own classroom. I never quite got in my comfort zone as an Instructional Coach. I regularly visited classrooms to observe and provided pointers and tips. It was a more laid back position, but I was never really comfortable in it. I didn't have a classroom to call my own. It made things awkward at times and sometimes I felt displaced, but I made the best of those next seven months and still found joy in working with the children and their teachers.

Out of the blue, we found out that Mrs. Teasley was being promoted to Principal of a nearby high school. I asked her to PLEASE take me with her to the high school, and that's exactly what she did. This takes me to Lyndell High School, the first all-black high school in my city. It's the high school my parents attended and where they met. I often visited there as a child and would follow my dad, who was a DJ, to spin records at high school dances. Wow had these last few years bought me "full circle".

I spent my last four years of teaching childcare at Lyndell High. This time around I worked along with two outstanding teachers Ms. Hill and Mr. Jones. They ran the Pre-kindergarten lab area. I no longer had to keep up with both areas (Pre-K and high school) of the classroom. This was a great change and we made an awesome team. Just like at Jacksonville, the "love affair" between Ms. Cofer and her students was back on. In fact, in those first few months, my students were the only other friendly faces that I saw. Let me explain. When Ms. Teasley arrived at Lyndell as Principal, the staff was not welcoming to her or to any of us that came with her. They were upset over losing their former principal, so it took me a little while to win them over. However, within a year or two, I had worked my charm so that by my last year of teaching, my co-workers once again voted me Teacher of the Year. Can you believe that? I had taught at three different schools and was named Teacher of the Year at all three. What a career and what a way to go out! I had some absolutely awesome students at Lyndell. I can't possibly name them because there are far too many. Students that do come to mind include Tamela, Kimmie, Vanessa, Dominica, Ivy Marie,

David, Brenna, Kiki, Harriet, Sharyl and Marvin. In fact, I still hear from Tamela, Kimmie, Dominica and David regularly. They were super special to me then, and still are now. I could easily write a chapter or two about each of these students. However, that would be another book! I started with the Lyndell class of 2013 when they were freshmen, and when they graduated, I retired.

10

A Lesson In Leadership

"Angels All Around"

From the very first day I began my teaching career, I was convinced that angels surrounded me and guided my every footstep. There were several angels stationed at every school I ever entered, and it appeared as though they all, ranging from students to parents, had their own distinct duty. They also included veteran teachers with years of knowledge and wisdom, new teachers that offered fresh new ideas, as well as principals that gave encouraging comments or constructive criticism. There are far too many to mention.

Over the 30+ years, I have worked with several different principals, and I feel very blessed and fortunate to have had them all. Each of them was unique and taught me valuable lessons. Most lessons were learned through positive experiences, while other lessons were learned from negative experiences. Regardless, I learned from these great "leaders." Although there were several, I would like to highlight five of them. I think I'll start off with my very first principal, Mr. Craften. I already mentioned him very early in the book because he was the principal who fought hard with the Board of Education to hire me. What made this so heroic is the fact that back in 1982, Richmond County was not hiring any "black" teachers, but Mr. Craften used his clout to get them to hire this "black" teacher. Although he was an older man, he had not lost his ability to run a school. So many principals today seem to be or want to be administrators just so that they can get out of the classroom. They have no clue as to what's going on in their school or how to successfully run a school.

Mr. Craften tolerated no misbehaving or disrespect. His hallways were always, and I do mean **always** orderly. He was visible and available. He called for students to come to their busses in such a way that as the children came down the hall, all you could see was one long straight line of kids headed to the loading zone. I had never seen anything like it. During lunch, the lunchroom was quiet, and I am not exaggerating. At his school, silent lunch actually meant silence.

Teachers felt safe because they knew that he had their back. He didn't have a whole lot of faculty meetings, but when he did, he got his point across. He didn't punish all teachers for something that one or two teachers did wrong. He was man enough to go directly to the teacher who needed "guidance" and politely "guide him or her." But whether giving guidance or praise, he was fair. Those were the days. He was a hands-on principal!

Mr. Smalls came to Kipling a few years after Mr. Craften retired. He was a young principal who stood behind his teachers. If teachers did their job, they had no problems from him. However, if they did not, he would step in and help them. He too, was very visible. He handled discipline problems immediately and often led the staff development workshops with teaching suggestions. He was a fun principal. Although he did not play discipline-wise with the kids, he had fun with them. He knew his kids and was full of energy. He often performed at assemblies or pep rallies. He didn't seem to pick favorites. He was easy to talk to and treated all teachers fairly. The only thing that I can think of that I disliked about him is that he only stayed one year. Because he was such a great leader, I hated to see him leave.

After only one year as an elementary school principal, Mr. Smalls was sent to be principal of a high school. As a matter of fact, he ended up being my daughter's principal at her high school. Once again he was loved by all. My daughter, as well as all of her peers, adored him. She often had conversations with him and he knew her by name. How rare is that these days - to know a student's name who never caused any problems? Boy did I hate to see him go, but I felt so blessed and safe to have him at my daughter's school.

Third on the list is Mr. Stanback. He was the first principal that I had when I arrived at the high school level. Upon arriving, a few days before school began, he met me at the vocational building and immediately started helping me bring in my classroom supplies. Right away I knew he was different. Up until this point, I hadn't moved much, but I never had a principal that helped me move "anything" without calling for a custodian. But Mr. Stanback was so helpful. From day one he always made me think of a man whose mom had "raised him right". He was not only nice to me, but he was nice to everyone and was loved by all. Under his reign, Jacksonville seemed to be on top of its game. He could get all of his staff members to do anything. On my very first day of school, there was an altercation in my classroom, and he immediately came from the front office, which was quite a distance, to my room on the other side of campus in the vocational building. He just wanted to make sure things were OK. He was a principal who was genuinely concerned about the welfare of others.

I would always refer to him as Reverend Stanback because during every pep rally or assembly he would give a speech that sounded like a sermon. All of our programs were spirit-filled. He would have most of the teachers and, even some of the students, on their feet and saying "Amen." He was easy to talk to, and he never changed. Now he didn't always agree with everybody, but he was so nice that even when he disagreed or said no, nobody got upset. Boy did we all hate to see him go. Luckily for me, Mr. Stanback and I attended the same church, so I still got to see him, hear him "preach", and enjoy his singing on a regular basis. **Lesson here: Never let your status change who you are.**

After Mr. Stanback left, Mrs. Teasley, who was his assistant principal, became Principal. She was the little lady with big ideas. My first encounter with her as an administrator was when I first arrived at Jacksonville. The Principal with a plan, she always seemed to have something on her mind. Usually it was some idea on how to make our students perform better academically. I had always heard that when she was a math teacher, she was the best. She took those same ideas from her classroom and used them to run the school. This was during the time when the Georgia High School Graduation Test was still sort of new, and she would dream up new ways to get students to pass those tests. She was a good Principal, but one thing that everyone knew about Mrs. Teasley was that she was "blunt". Whatever was on her mind, she would let you know. She was not concerned about one's feelings or how what she said sounded. She said it and then she was through with it. Strictly business, she did not hold things against anyone and would easily encourage those who felt offended. For those who were sensitive and wanted to stay upset or angry about one of her statements, that was up to them, but as for Mrs. Teasley, she had moved on.

The good part about her was that no matter how disappointed or upset she was, she would never hurt anyone. She wanted the best for her students and faculty. The students loved her also, and she knew all 450+ by name. Now that's special.

I cannot finish my discussion about Mrs. Teasley without mentioning one of the biggest lessons she taught me. One of the most humbling experiences I had as a teacher happened as a result of one of Mrs. Teasley's lessons. This situation involved a young man named Jamie. He was placed in my classroom during his junior year of high school and my first year of teaching high school. He was loud, wild, loved to be seen, and always wanted things his way. Up until that time, there had only been one way in my classroom, and that was my way. Somehow, I made it through the school year and I was glad to see him go.

The next school year began and there I was praying my second year would be filled with nice, calm students who could follow rules. Well, in walks Mrs. Teasley who **told** me, not asked me, to take Jamie back because he needed this class to graduate. My heart dropped! There I stood giving her reason after reason why he should find another class and there she was still telling me, like it or not, he was returning. Boy, did she put something on my mind. No matter what I thought or how I felt about Jamie, he would be back in my class, and she expected him to pass because he was highly capable. I believe it was at that very moment, I realized what constituted real teaching.

Real teaching is unconditional. It is teaching no matter what, even if it means finding ways to make the most "awkward situation" work. It's not about proving yourself, getting the last word, or being right all the time. Defeat is not an option! It wasn't easy but I turned the other cheek and made that situation with Jamie work!!! And did it ever work. He came back and ran the lab, becoming one of my better teachers. The preschool kids loved him, and he and I ended up getting along great. It was all because I realized I was not right all the time and could not always have my way. Remaining confident and firm, I also allowed him to be himself without fighting him every step of the way. I also gave him choices within my choice range. This eventually made him "lighten up" and understand me and my ways better.

Jamie was probably my first real lesson upon arriving at Jacksonville High. The ordeal with him was just a practice session for all of my babies that came behind him. Good Ole Ms. Teasley taught me how to calm down and just **"do what I do"**. Nothing more, nothing less. I do believe she was one of the main reasons for my success on the high school level.

Finally, there was Dr. Cason! Not there to be a friend, she was there to work and that was what she wanted from her teachers. Now, people had many different opinions about "Doc"; however, I wasn't really concerned about that. I had no issues. I did my job and we got along great. SHE DID NOT PLAY and the kids understood that. This made my job easy.

So there's my spill on some of my principals. These five principals have truly been my angels. They all expected their teachers to do their job and if teachers did, their jobs were usually stress free. They didn't worry about going around acting or trying to prove that they were the boss. They simply allowed their teachers to do their jobs. I thank God for them all. There were a few more principals that I worked under, and they were also great; however, if I tried to write about them all, that would be another entire book!

11

A Lesson In Family Ties

Throughout this book I have mentioned many experiences and many children. There are two, or should I say three, children that I have not discussed yet but are extremely important to me: my daughter Chanita, a.k.a "Nita", my son Reginald G., a.k.a "Brother", and my husband Reginald H. Where can I start?

Chanita Re'Ne Cofer

Well, Nita my daughter was that little girl that was born my second year of teaching. Quite a funny little girl, she was born with light hazel eyes like her dad and grew up to have a low alto voice. As a child, she was very active from day one and spent almost every day away from her parents. All this child ever wanted to do was go to

Grandma Shirley's. At the age of four, we enrolled her into daycare. That child cried every single day for an entire month. She even started making up stories about the teacher; stories like "the teacher kicked me." Finally, after a month she was a "drop out." Yeah my Chanita was one of the youngest "drop outs" in the county. So once again she was happy, Grandma Shirley was happy, and even Great-Grandma Nancy, who kept her every day, was happy. As for me, I could finally stop wondering whether or not Chanita would still be crying when I arrived at the daycare at the end of the day. The following year when she went to kindergarten, she went to her classroom, told me goodbye, and never cried about going to school ever again. Now, this really shocked me because up until this point, I had always thought that a child had to have some type of experience in a school setting with other children in order for them to adjust socially in "real school". Well, Chanita dismissed all of these beliefs and became a "social butterfly."

I distinctly remember Chanita being in third grade and her teacher consistently having her students read in front of the class. By the end of that year, Chanita was able to talk to anyone, anywhere, anytime. She never, ever met a stranger. Having had great elementary years, she never had any discipline problems and made very good grades. Of course, I had very strict rules at home and she knew not to have discipline problems at school. Sometimes I felt like I slighted my own children, because there were times I was so exhausted from working hard that I wasn't able to do my best with my own children. Nonetheless, Chanita did fine, which is remarkable, because during her elementary years I had two jobs where I taught day and night. Her middle school and high school years were also decent. She began playing violin in elementary. She eventually began playing piano by ear, and later started saxophone in middle school. She joined the bands in both middle school and high school, and was voted "most talented" by her senior class in high school.

Each and every day throughout Chanita's high school years she would come to my room, after school, and give me a minute by minute summary of her day. Again, not one time was I ever called to the school for misbehavior, and I am most proud of this. She ended up qualifying for the HOPE Scholarship and went to college. She finished with a major and minor degree, along with membership into Delta Sigma Theta Sorority Inc. from my Alma Mater, Georgia Southern University. She is a hard worker and now owns her own home.

Reginald Gordon Cofer, Better Known as Brother

I guess I'll start off telling you why he is called "Brother". When my son, Reginald G. was born, his sister, Chanita absolutely adored him and still does. She would sit and look at him or hold him for hours a day calling him "My Brother Baby." So over time, everyone in the family began calling him "Brother Baby." After a few years of this, "Brother Baby" was no longer a baby, so we simply dropped off the "Baby" and he became everybody's "Brother."

Brother was my calmer child, but he hated to go to sleep. Unlike his sister, who was not so calm and could fall asleep in the middle of a conversation. From the very first night home from the hospital, he fought sleep and this continued until high school. Anyway, he was much calmer than his sister, who was always on some type of adventure. At an early age, Brother could sit and stay focused on an activity for quite a while. However, whenever his sister was around, she could get him to do just about anything. In fact, when Chanita first started school, my Mom would always say "Brother would be fine until Chanita got home." (Chanita always had a "special control" over Grandma Shirley.)

Brother's elementary school days were also good, and he never had discipline problems. Middle and high school were pretty good for him as well. However, during his junior year, I transferred him to Jacksonville with me during the Christmas break. Even though his grades were good at the other high school, something just wasn't right because he did not seem to enjoy high school like most students. In late October, he even told me that some of his teachers still didn't know his name. I brought him over to my school, and he never looked back or even thought about his old high school again.

Brother and I had a ball. We would ride to Jacksonville every morning, usually listening to all kinds of music which ranged from Luther Barnes to Prince. I would sing, which was one of my favorite hobbies, and he would listen. We rode home each day and talked about our day and how much fun our day had been. He never, ever wanted to miss a day of school after enrolling at Jacksonville. He was definitely "feeling the love". Prior to leaving his other high school, he wondered whether or not he would fit in, but the kids at Jacksonville were so accepting that fitting-in came naturally. He absolutely fell in love with that school, and I immediately saw a difference. Suddenly my shy, quiet, reserved child was becoming just as outgoing as his sister. He joined the Coach Reese's Eagles Basketball Team and was well-loved by his teammates and school mates. Reggie ended up being number five in his senior class and he, too, qualified for the HOPE scholarship. After graduation, he enrolled at Georgia Southern University, also, rooming with his sister for the first few years and graduating with a degree in communications.

I truly believe that my teaching career helped me greatly with raising my children. While at Jacksonville, I had a chance to have him in my childcare class, which was quite an experience. He was an "outstanding" student with book work. The lab was another story. Our lab consisted of teaching preschoolers, which he did well.; however, the cleaning up afterwards needed some work. I placed him with a group of girls who gave him no slack. They had him cleaning and mopping before he knew what hit him. Thank God for those group members. The experience of teaching my child was quite pleasant.

I learned a lot while raising my biological children. Although I was very firm and spanked them sometimes, I never used insults or profanity while disciplining them. This really seemed to make them very pleasant children. Even though I can't say that both of them are "curse free", (I'll let you figure out which one probably uses profanity); nevertheless, I always get compliments about how well-behaved and nice they are. **Some of the lessons learned from my children include the following… (1) The best way to teach a child is by example.** Children are always watching us and it is very important for adults to always carry themselves in a responsible manner because children don't just do as we say, but they are more likely to do as we do. **(2) Don't send your kids to church; take them with you.** From birth I have always made sure that my children attended church regularly. At very young ages, they both joined the church, were baptized, and became active in the church. As they grew older, they eagerly arrived at some church events before I did. Even today my children sit near the front of the church, while I sit closer to the back, and they never have to be forced to attend. They look forward to it. **(3) Consistency has proven to be key, and being consistent really paid off in the classroom and while raising my children.** Consistency leaves no room for confusion. It leads to habits, good and bad. Consistent positive guidance yields good habits, and consistent negative guidance yields bad habits. **(4) Learn your children and parent accordingly.** Every child is different and shouldn't be compared to the other. I couldn't discipline Chanita the same way that I did Brother. But they both know that they are loved enormously and are equally special. **(5) Everyone has talents. Some are very visible and some discreet.** Both of my children have their own very special and unique talents. Chanita is the child who can handle business. She plays beautiful music with her saxophone, piano, or violin, she never forgets a face or name, she has quick wit when it comes to joking, and she writes well and draws pretty decently. Brother cannot handle business as well, but he has a vocabulary out of this world, draws beautifully, has outstanding comprehension, and gets up in front of a crowd on short notice and speaks so eloquently. These very different personalities require me to "parent" each of them differently. I am proud of these two adults that we have raised. They have grown into kind, patient, compassionate, generous, and spiritual individuals. Chanita's active personality has evolved into making her a real go-getter. She loves to talk and uses this to her advantage. Brother is very methodical in all that he does. Nothing seems to make him speed up and he has a stubborn streak; however, he is never disrespectful when showing either side. I truly thank God for such well-behaved children. Working with children every day, I insisted that my children not give their teachers the problems that some of my students gave me.

Remember, I mentioned earlier that my children taught me a lot, so in no way do I mean to indicate that I did everything right, because I didn't. I tried, but I'm not perfect. Well.....moving on to ...

My True Love, Reginald H. Cofer

Sometimes referred to as my oldest child, he enjoys playing just as much, if not more, as any child I know. I was first introduced to Reginald, my husband when I was twelve years old at a wrestling match. Yes, I said a wrestling match. Each Monday night at the Bell Auditorium, our local entertainment coliseum, my cousins, some girlfriends, and I would go to watch wrestling. Well, one particular evening my cousin Peggy and her best friend Susie - they were the oldest in our group - decided to "set me up" with a boyfriend. Susie had a cousin that worked at the Bell Auditorium, and thought we would be a good match for each other. I thought he was cute; however, he thought that I was a "little girl". He was polite and took my number but never called.

Oh well!!! A few months later I began my first year of high school at no other than Jacksonville High School, and who did I run into during my fifth period math class? The young man who thought I was a "little girl". We became fast friends and after a few months, Reg simply stopped bringing his book to class which gave us an excuse to share books. It took almost the entire year, but by spring we were a couple. I actually believe that, for me, this connection with Reginald was "love at first sight". What I didn't know about Reg when I met him, is that he was an "outstanding" athlete and very, very, very competitive. He played football, basketball, and baseball, and he played all of them well. I had been a cheerleader since sixth grade, so I continued cheering in high school. It was a lot of fun cheering, especially cheering for the "best player" on the team! From ninth grade until the age of 22, Reginald and I dated. He received a full basketball scholarship to Georgia Southern College, which is now Georgia Southern University. He convinced me to attend also. He majored in Communications and I majored in Early Childhood Education. Although there were a few rough spots in our relationship during those nine years, our relationship was great and still is. I consider Reginald to be my best friend and I have always thought of him as just a highly intelligent, nice, respectful man with beautiful eyes. I could go on and on, but that too would be a whole "notha" book. I will say this though, throughout our relationship, Reginald has taught me a few lessons. **One lesson was to not worry over things that you cannot control and also that you cannot please everyone.**

Two things that we as parents never did was go against each other. Once one parent made a decision, that was it. And we never argued in front of our children, although we really don't argue much at all. If we did argue, we did it when the children were not present. I am certain that this is why our children never argue with each other and rarely, if ever, have "ugly" disagreements with anyone (that I know of). However, I will admit that Chanita can be provoked much easier than her brother. Well anyway that's an update on my immediate family.

Over the years, they have all been patient with me listening to story after story about the many adventures of Cheryl's day at work. Some great – others OK – and then others, very few, not so good.

12

A Lesson In Gratefulness

Well, it's been more than fifteen years since I began writing about my career. It started as just journal writing. I was just sitting at home one day and realized how much I loved teaching. Through all the good and the bad, I was blessed to become a teacher. The funny thing about this is that even though I was always interested in teaching, it was not my first career choice. As far back as I can remember, I always loved to sing and dance. I've always been surrounded by music. My dad sings and he and my mom founded and opened a record store in the 70's which he still owns today. Also, many of my days were spent with my "big" cousins, Katy, also a teacher, and DeeDee. Katy and Dee Dee are actually my mom's first cousins, but felt like our big sisters. They were our regular babysitters as kids. You could say they helped raise us. With them there, I can remember being introduced to the Chil-lites and other great sounds of the 70's. I loved, and still do love, all types of music. It could be gospel, blues, or soul, and as I got older, even now, hip-hop or rap.

My favorite musicians as a child ranged from Aretha Franklin to the Jackson Five. If they had recorded a song, I could sing it. I just knew that one day I'd be on a stage like them. As a young girl growing up, I can remember my sister, some other cousins, and me pretending that our side porch was our stage. Now let me tell you about these cousins, The Phillips Cousins. There were three girls (Peggy, MeMe, and Johnica) and two boys (Dwayne and Lee). The girls were close to our age. One summer they moved to Georgia from Florida right across the street from us. We had never seen each other before, and after watching each other for weeks and finally becoming acquainted, we became inseparable. We would sing from sun up to sun down.

Out of all of "us" cousins, my cousin Peggy and I were into the music more than the rest. She and I even worked in my parent's record store together, and usually spent ALL of our earnings buying music. Peggy was a "real" musician and still is. She sings and plays several instruments. We just couldn't get it out of our system. We would sit around for hours listening to her play song after song on the piano. Peggy ended up being an excellent and experienced musician. Although she reads music, she can also play anything she hears on piano, organ, clarinet, or guitar. She has been fortunate enough to play in several of our local churches. These congregations are blessed to have her. To this day we are still very close. About once per week, we have our long talks that are very inspiring. In fact, she was a major inspiration for most of this book. I have always thought that musicians have a different way of thinking, myself included. The talks that Peggy and I have always enhanced my way of thinking. She, her two sisters, my sister, and I are extremely close. In fact, the five of us are just like sisters. Two other cousins that I grew up with and remain close to are Tania and Teesa. We have been as thick as thieves since junior high. I can still count on them for anything to this day. All of my cousins played major roles in my life. I cannot imagine them not being in my life, and I thank God for all of them.

But back to me, unfortunately, singing was something that I only did behind closed doors for years because I became "chicken" as I grew up. I would sing along with every song I heard when I was at home or in my car but not in front of anyone. Eventually, I did join some church choirs. Maybe now that I have retired, I can do more singing in public. Anyway, I settled for teaching and have never regretted it.

Teaching became so habit forming that it did not feel like a job. This would become part of one of my famous quotes passed on to my students. The quote simply states, **"Find a career that you love because when you enjoy your work, it does not feel like work."**

There are so many, many people and events that have helped to make my teaching experience so wonderful. So many that I don't know where to begin. In fact, I am certain that if I tried to name them all, I would definitely leave someone out. I will simply say thanks to all of my wonderful parents, co-workers, principals, classroom volunteers, family members, in-laws, friends and especially my students. You have all helped to make my teaching career "Simply the best"!!!!!!!!

I would also like to thank my step father, and grandparents, aunt, sister, and parents. They have always supported EVERYTHING that I have ever done in my life, both at home and at work. All of these family members taught me great work ethics and also showed me unconditional love. I could probably write an entire book on each of them, but will elaborate on my parents, aunt and sister instead.

I'll start with my dad, Robert Francis "Flash" Gordon. Although I was not in the same house as my dad after the age of 12, he is an awesome dad. He always worked hard and provided well for our family. The major things that I developed from him are the absolute love of music and showing initiative in all that I do. As stated earlier, there was always music in my home. We had all kinds of music and my dad has an amazing voice. I can remember many times hearing him singing in perfect harmony with music that was being played in our home. This is something that I do as well. I may not sing with the music in perfect harmony, but I do sing with just about every song that I hear. I do this so much that my husband often asks me "Can we please hear the real song this time?" Dad always says that music is our friend. It allows you be free and enjoy other things you like, unlike the television that keeps you confined to one area. Which brings me to the word **Initiative**. This is my absolute most favorite word!!! I don't think he even realized it, but my dad taught me all about the word initiative. My first paying job was at the Big "G" Platter Shop. This was a record store founded by my mother and father. I spent my summers working there. When there were no customers to wait on, Daddy made sure that there was no sitting around. There was ALWAYS something that needed to be done. There was straightening, dusting, window washing, restocking, cleaning, and the list goes on. It was as though he hated to see you relaxing. I didn't understand then, but I later learned that this practice certainly pays off. It helps you stay organized and ahead of the game, and it keeps your surroundings in order and appealing. Initiative was the first word I taught my high school students each year. After just a few weeks in my class, it was quickly understood that there was always work to be done in Mrs. Cofer's classroom. This not only pertained to my students, but to myself as well. Often, my students would say to me, "Mrs. Cofer, do you ever sit down?" It helped me stay organized and ahead of the game. I'd like to thank my dad for this great gift!!!!

There is s-o-o-o-o-o much that I could say about my mother, but I am certain to leave something out because that would definitely be "another book". Never have I EVER, EVER, EVER met a person like her. She is truly an amazing person and my inspiration. My mother, Shirley Grier, is the strongest and smartest woman that I know. All of my life, I have known that there is nothing that she would not do for her children. She taught my sister and me to have high self-esteem and to be independent. We were also taught to be kind to others and to be selfless. For as long as I can remember, my mother has given selflessly to help others in addition to her children. She is also a fighter, not physically, but for what's right. This could sometimes get out of hand, but always with good intentions. Mother just has a hard time holding her tongue when things don't seem fair.

Finally, she is a survivor. NOTHING knocks her down, at least not for long. Not even cancer. When she was in her late 20's, she was diagnosed with breast cancer. Breast cancer for one in her twenties was something rarely heard of in the 60s, but here she is, over fifty years later, still here. What more can I say?

My auntie, Thomasina Grant, is absolutely one of the funniest, most creative, and sweetest people that I know. I had the pleasure of working with her at my very first teaching job. What a blessing! It was like having my mother right there at the job with me. She had already been teaching for several years, so I learned greatly just by watching her. From her, I immediately learned that love and laughter are both very important in a classroom. She was the type of teacher that never seemed to let anything bother her or allow anything to ruin her day, which is rather hard to do in a classroom setting. She was stern when she needed to be, but afterward she was right back showing love and making her classroom a fun, learning environment. I truly feel it was her deep passion for the profession that inspired me to become a teacher.

Lastly, I cannot complete this section without saying a little more about my sister, Pamela. She is the best! She is definitely one in a million. For as long as I can remember she has been my best friend. She is one of the most compassionate, intelligent, and sweetest people I know. How blessed I am to have a sister like her. I can always depend on her. I guess if I were to put it in today's language, she'd be "my ride or die"! My sister is a lot like my mom and probably is the stronger of the two of us. However, we are as different as day and night and it has been that way for as far as I can remember. She's the stylish sister and I'm the jeans and sweat pants sister. She likes to "party all the time", while I prefer a quiet evening. She is high-spirited and I am rather reserved. She is an early riser and I can sleep until noon. Pamela loves a convertible. I love a sedan. I think you get the picture. However, there is one thing that we do have in common and that is our love for each other.

13

Conclusion

I guess by now you can tell it has taken me more than fifteen years to complete this memoir. Looking back over my thirty-two year teaching career, several things flood my mind. The teaching profession has drastically changed. This is probably due in part to the changes of our times. Schools have changed because the people that we serve have changed. Teachers are no longer "automatically" respected. Talking back to explain themselves or cursing, as if no adult is present, are everyday behaviors for children both "young and old".

Budget cuts have made it difficult for teachers to properly do their jobs without using hundreds of dollars out of their own pockets. These cuts result in minimal classroom supplies and materials, thus, making instruction sometimes suffer.

From all of these memories, adventures, and experiences, one thing I feel certain of is that twenty-five to thirty years of teaching is enough - and I mean this in the most positive way. I still feel qualified and effective, but would it be fair to the children in the classroom to continue teaching? I am generations away from them and a lot has happened to our education system in the last thirty years; Students have changed, parents have changed, teachers have changed, and the school system has changed.

What kind of student changes have I seen? These changes in no way include "EVERYONE". I guess the biggest change is the lack of "automatic" respect. Back in the day, if you were a teacher, respect meant something to everybody, and teachers were admired and respected by all. Not anymore. Students now will say anything they want to say to teachers and some students are outright rude (talking back and cursing them) to teachers. Most students use curse words, in general, not to be rude, but as a part of their daily language, even at the elementary level. Some students do anything in front of their teachers. I would never let my boyfriend put his arm around me in front of a teacher, but now they hug and kiss wherever they feel like it. More bullying is going on now more than ever before. In an age run by technology, bullying is easier to do than ever. Also, not as many students take pride in their work anymore, and many students have to be begged to complete assignments. Computers and computer games have taken over! Cursive writing and telling time on a clock with a minute and hour hand are things of the past.

Parents used to trust teachers. If there was an issue with a student, when I first started teaching, you could bet that the parent would **never** defy the teacher. Nowadays, parents will come to the school to "get you straight" about their child. Some mean well. Others do not. Some are involved in working to try to provide for their family and others are not. There seems to be a new style of parenting. This style of parenting involves very little discipline. Some parents (not all) often don't hold their children accountable for their actions. Parents don't talk to their children as much. Children are allowed to be babysat by an IPad. Unfortunately, some changes are due to the fact that many teachers have changed.

With all of these new changes that have manifested, the new-style teachers are needed to come in and take over for the traditional teacher. The teacher that is closer to their generation and can understand or "feel" them. In 1982, I was that new-style teacher and I was what worked for that time, but thirty years later, I need to step aside. For one thing, it's hard for the older teacher to adapt to these changes. Moreover, a lot of the things that worked in the 80's are no longer effective though some older teachers are still trying to use them. Now I'm not saying that "we" old heads can no longer be effective or that we are all washed out. I am certain that I can still be quite effective; however, I have had to be open to lots of changes. Many veterans cannot and will not change. There are those veterans, like me, who still eat, drink, and breathe teaching and are willing to go the extra mile. However, there are also those that are just simply going through the motions. This is a sure sign of "It's time to go!" I can't possibly speak for all, but I believe a thirty year or possibly thirty-five year career of serious teaching is enough for most teachers because after that, children are being handicapped.

I have made my teaching days seem as though they were all "GREAT"!!!! They weren't. There were times when things definitely did not go as I had planned. That's when I would step back, re-evaluate myself and try something else. Never, ever did I want to reconsider the career that I had chosen.

Well, I could probably go on and on about my teaching experiences..... probably for an eternity...... However, I think I'll simply wrap up things with some of my favorite quotes and suggestions. Some new and some not so new. Here goes......

14

Cheryl's Top Suggestions

1. Leave lazy at home. Give teaching your best each and every day. Show Initiative. Teaching is not for everyone!!!! If you can't give it your best most of the time, it might NOT be for you.

2. Create a homelike atmosphere in your classroom.

3. Keep your classroom clean. Purchase your own cleaning materials and supplies. Use them regularly. Do not depend on others to keep your classroom clean.

4. Organize your teaching materials. Know where things are.

5. Show unconditional love and respect every day. This is a must.

6. Learn/know your students and teach them accordingly. (This may be my favorite suggestion). Find their interests and capitalize on it.

7. Learn names ASAP (preferably day 1 or 2), no later than Week One. Make it personal for each student. Relationships are super important. Start Day 1 to find something unique and/or "the good" in "each" child.

8. Learn (GET TO KNOW) your students and your parents. Make an effort to make some type of contact with each child's parent early. Nothing builds the parent-teacher relationship like a first of the year phone call (contact) to introduce yourself and your class and let the parent know how excited you are to be teaching their child. Calling parents before there is a problem makes most parents more supportive when you have to call for an actual problem. Also, keep them informed on a regular basis.

9. Take care of your responsibilities. Be professional and positive. Keep accurate records and documentation. Plan and over plan appropriately.

10. Stay in your lane.

11. SET your rules. REVIEW, REVIEW, REVIEW. Say what you mean and MEAN what you say. Do not make promises you KNOW you can not keep. In the heat of the moment, do not threaten them with something that you have no intention or authority to implement. If this is done correctly in the beginning, your class will run itself after the first month. (Boy are you 'gonna be worn out that first month). "Most" kids do what you allow them to do and they figure that out pretty quickly. Let them know (by your actions) that they will get tired before you will.

12. Realize that you cannot force a person to do anything he or she does not want to do. Never take misbehavior "personally"! Even though it may seem as though that child is acting out

against you, you are probably the last thing on their mind. Tomorrow will probably be better.

13. Do not forget "Old School". Technology is great.....BUT, Parents and Teachers should allow kids to take Technology Breaks. Allow them to take part in "old school" learning. Things like telling time without a digital clock, counting real money and making change without a machine, writing in cursive, etc.

14. When you get a student that seems impossible, and it makes you ask yourself "what in the WORLD am I going to do with him or her?" LET your answer be....I guess I'll love and teach him/her.

15. Do not be ashamed to ask other teachers questions or suggestions on what works for them.

16. Do not be ashamed to asked friends and loved ones for support: Getting organized and buying treats cost money.

17. Stay OUT of the teacher's lounge!

18. Remember, YOU determine how your day goes - meaning you know what pushes that child's buttons. Ask yourself, "Do I want to go down that road today?"

19. Go to church, stay prayerful, and take the Lord in the building with you every day, even if you are the only one who knows He's there.

20. FINALLY, realize what you have......a good job (maybe not the best in the world, but a good one with great benefits and holidays). And remember that one or two bad days do not make the job bad. Where else can you get that many days off your FIRST year on the job? AND LOOK AT ALL THE LOVE YOU GET!!!!!!! OMG.

Although no career or job situation is perfect, there are some that do come pretty close. Just try to remember "You" can determine how your day goes. Most of our outcomes are determined by how we react to the situation. This book simply contains things that worked for me. I am certain that my stories are very similar to things most teachers do. I truly believe that this book, along with an optimistic attitude, can possibly be the guide to a successful teaching career or any career/situation involving people. Until next time, I hope you will enjoy YOUR journey as much as I have enjoyed mine.

Made in USA - Kendallville, IN
1172193_9781725052154
09.29.2020 1104